SHOOT-OUT AT SALT FLAT

To Dave,
A west Texas thriller.
Warm regards,
Lynn M. Chelewski
Oct 3, 2015

By Lynn Chelewski

Cover illustration by Bonnie Curnock
Interior illustration by Mike Capron

First published by Dog Ear Publishing
4010 W. 86th Street, Ste H
Indianapolis, IN 46268
www.dogearpublishing.net

ISBN: 978-1-4575-2507-0

This book is printed on acid-free paper.

Printed in the United States of America

To the memory of Roger E. Reisch
February 6, 1924–February 12, 2013

Roger Reisch was the first and only employee of Guadalupe Mountains National Park in the West Texas panhandle back in the 1960s. In a literal sense, he was the Lone Ranger!

He was born in St. Louis, Missouri, and it was there that he was buried 89 years later. He actually died in Edmond, Oklahoma, but his body was returned to St. Louis to be buried in the family plot. I was a pallbearer at his funeral, traveling from Southeast Nebraska and narrowly dodging a blizzard. At Roger's funeral, his nephew Jim Reisch commented that it didn't seem right, having the funeral in St. Louis, as for most all of his life, his association with Uncle Roger had been with far West Texas and the Guadalupe Mountains. Sometimes, the logistics of life, time, and location change things. Unfortunately, I was the only National Park Service (NPS) veteran who knew Roger who was present at his funeral, and the only current-duty NPS staff was a close personal friend of mine, Laura Stresemann, who worked in St. Louis at Jefferson National Memorial Exapansion,or "the Arch" as many prefer to call it. Had Roger's funeral been in Carlsbad, New Mexico, there would no doubt have been a huge number in attendance. It was indeed a long way from Texas when he was laid to rest on that rainy, chilly day in St. Louis.

Because Roger, eccentricities aside, was so giving, it was fitting that some of whom he blessed and inspired were able to return the favor in a small way upon his death. When his brother, "Jack," contacted me to let me know that he was having trouble finding a full dress uniform for Roger from all the boxes of stuff he had in storage, the solution was only a few keystrokes away. I had a dress shirt, tie, tie tack, and belt I could donate, and a friend of mine, Vidal Davila, who was superintendent at Wind Cave NM in South Dakota, donated a dress coat, and the rest was provided by Dennis Vasquez, the superintendent at Guadalupe Mountains. I was honored to do such a small favor, because in many ways, Roger had given me the shirt off of his back over the years.

Although there is no character centered around Roger in this novel, the fact that the novel is intrinsically centered on, even interwoven around, the Guadalupe Mountains is enough reason to dedicate it to him. He was back in the day known as "Mr. Guadalupe Mountains," a tag that I am sure he took great pride in until his dying day. The only semblance Roger bears to the central character in the novel is that Roger was a Marine Corps veteran, as am I. I enlisted at the end of the Viet Nam era; Roger served in WWII and for a while during the Korean Conflict. The biggest percentage of his adult life, however, was in the NPS, a career he started with a career-conditional appointment back in May 2, 1960. Although he served at a number of National Park Sites, the bulk of his career was at Guadalupe Mountains National Park. What he didn't explore by pickup truck or jeep, he did so on horseback or on foot. He was a man of many interests, particularly history, botany, and biology. More than that, Roger appreciated people—and likewise, they appreciated him, despite his many eccentrics .

If I had chosen to create a character based on Roger, the entire dynamics of *The Shootout at Salt Flat* would have changed. The book was a work in progress during Roger's last couple of years, and although he never was privy to reading the manuscript, it seems only fitting to dedicate it to his memory.

Roger was a man who revered the great outdoors that God created: the beautiful topography, flora and fauna within, and the flowing streams of crystal-clear water, which might as well be molten silver, for water is so valuable in this delicate desert environment. He loved and doted on his horses, having purchased several of them along with tack gear and donated them to the park for use. In the photo, he is mounted on Blackjack at the top of Bear Canyon in 1972. One who is familiar with horses and tack gear will note that Blackjack is wearing a hackamore, not a bit and bridle, which he despised. Roger was sensitive to these things, even in animals—so much so that he once nominated another of his horses, Alejandro, for a performance award in relocating some wild turkeys into the backcountry. Superintendent Bill Dunmire later presented that award to Roger and his horse; the descendents of those turkeys inhabit the backcountry of the park to this day.

After his retirement and relocation to be with family in St. Louis, Missouri, and later near Oklahoma City, Oklahoma, Roger sustained an interest and passion for the Guadalupes and for West Texas and Southeast New Mexico. The last thing he donated to the park from his private collection was a lensatic compass. He had used it for navigating the mountains with a topographical map back in the old days. To many of us, Roger Reisch *was that compass*—a guide who pointed the way on many things pertaining to the preservation, appreciation, and respect for one of our great national treasures in this great United States of America.

So much could and *should* be written about Roger Reisch, but that merits a book of its own. He was certainly one of the last of the old-school NPS rangers. Suffice it to say that we were fast friends since meeting in 1986 and that this world, to us who knew him, is a less desirable place without him. He left a unique void that no one else can fill, and where he trod, the tenacious West Texas winds continue to howl and blow.

—Lynn Chelewski March 25, 2013

Foreword

In Texas, and particularly in the west where this story is set, travel is measured in hours, and the vistas stretch to the horizon or the next range of mountains. Dry lake beds called playas commonly occupy the lowest valleys, only rarely to fill with water after rainy periods, often years apart.

Folks who live in or travel through this desert land do not often enter the higher mountain areas that rise from the sparsely vegetated plains, often thousands of feet, and are covered with pine, Douglas fir, oaks, and even quaking aspen trees.

The lower elevation desert land is occupied by plants protected by spines, moisture-conserving coated leaves, or the fleshy skin of cacti. They mostly have shallow root structures that quickly capture any rain or morning dew, then slow down its loss from evaporation or transpiration.

In the mountains, the size and numbers of plants change with elevation, higher rainfall, and snow accumulation. In these cooler, higher elevations there is more moisture trapped by passing clouds, there are springs and even some flowing streams hidden in this forested vastness. Even on the shady, cooler north-facing slopes where there is less evaporation of precious water, much larger plants thrive. Here at the southern end of the Rocky Mountain chain, this basin and range country has forests of pine, fir, Douglas fir, oaks, and even aspen in the shaded, cooler canyons thousands of feet above the desert, existing as relic forests, surviving remnants from a much wetter, cooler time when glaciers covered the lands hundreds of miles to the north.

These areas also served as home for ancient and even historic native populations, and signs of their occupancy remain in the pictograph rock paintings, petroglyphs, cooking middens, stone shelters, and tepee rings. Legends of lost gold, Indian origins, lost wagon trains, Spanish conquistadors, stage coach robberies, and pioneer feuds have been part of the local lore and all of this became a familiar part of the author's knowledge in his years working, hiking, and camping in the wild desert and mountain country of the Guadalupe Mountains of Texas.

Author Lynn Chelewski grew to know the neighbors who ranched and farmed the area before it became a national park, was acquainted with Apache whose ancestors called this place home before being driven onto reservations by the Negro Buffalo Soldiers of the U.S. Cavalry, there to protect the influx of pioneering Anglos and Hispanics who next settled these rugged lands. Those who believe and are sensitive to the spiritual aspects of this wild country, and when traveling alone, may feel a special connection/communication with the land, the spaciousness, and the unspoken uplifting of the inner spirit a human being can experience in wild country, desert or mountain.

Today's residents of these desert and mountain environments are hardy, often descendants of families who have lived off the land as ranchers, farmers, or service providers to the small, far-flung desert and mountain communities for generations. These folks are hardy, often self-sufficient, and enjoy the lonelier lifestyle that comes with the vast emptiness and stark beauty of this West Texas country. They understand, expect, and respect the often harsh conditions of the land they have chosen, receive help from and provide it to neighbors when needed, carefully use and jealously protect the precious underground waters for their farms, and measure their livestock grazing needs by number of head per section of land instead of per acre as in the well-watered areas of our nation. Their lands are jealously protected from casual or other entry by outside folks and they proudly maintain their hardy lifestyle and rural manner, mostly with a politeness that one only infrequently finds in urban communities anymore.

In this, his first novel and mystery, author and friend of the West Lynn Chelewski has successfully captured the essence of this West Texas landscape, its people and their personalities and lifestyles. He has crafted an intricate tale of murder, love, greed, and injustice, the lives of the personalities involved, as well the history, natural history, legends, and mysteries of the ancients who still frequent these lands they once dominated. Chelewski uses the history and natural history and legends of this area he knows so well to paint the scenes in the reader's mind and bring them to life. Chelewski, a retired National Park Service employee and Marine Corps veteran, has through his writing reflected his love and knowledge of the land and his familiarity with its stories from the past, his sensitivity to political, land, water, and wildlife management issues and the effects of climate change, and his understanding of the people and relationships in the rural West Texas communities.

Lynn Chelewski served in the U.S. Marine Corps in the 1970s and joined the National Park Service at Padre Island National Seashore in 1982, later serving at Olympic National Park, Washington, Guadalupe Mountains National Park, Texas, Fort Larned National Historic Site, Kansas, again at Guadalupe Mountains, and culminating his National Park Service career at Homestead National Monument of America in Nebraska in 2003.

The author was the recipient of a number of National Park Service Special Achievement, Special Act, and Performance Awards during his career. His varied work experiences led to special recognition for development and directing a Symposium on the African American Military Experience (Buffalo Soldiers), training facilitator for National Park Service Employee Orientation, National Safety Council International Advisory Committee for Defensive Driving, and construction leader for the Ridley Sea Turtle Laboratory at Padre Island National Seashore, as well as teaching safety and interpretation classes, and leadership in environmental and equal opportunity initiatives. The author and his family currently reside in Nebraska.

—Larry E. Henderson
National Park Service Superintendent (Retired)
Guadalupe Mountains National Park

CHAPTER 1

Fading into the sunlight

The blazing sun was glaring off the arid expanse of salt lakes at the base of the Guadalupe Mountains in far West Texas. A red-tailed hawk soaring several thousand feet up near the vertical drop of that massive limestone edifice called El Capitan in the Guadalupe Mountains spied a lanky, six-foot-tall, brown-haired, bearded cowboy arriving in a rattling truck and a trail of dust. A Judy Collins tune, *Someday Soon,* was playing on the radio of the old pickup truck. "*...Just out of the service, and he's looking for his fun, someday soon, going with him someday soon...*"

Joe Mack pulled his beat up '52 Chevy pickup truck off to the side of the fence line and took a moment while he contemplated the roll of barbed wire and cedar fence stays in the back. Methodically he unsnapped his shirt pocket and fished out a cigarette, lighting it and taking in a slow drag as he squinted at the harsh, Chihuahuan Desert landscape. He flipped his Zippo lighter shut with a metallic click; it was a carry-over accessory from a vice he'd picked up in Viet Nam and hadn't been able to shake any more than his horrific memories from there.

"No sense rushing this little project," he commented aloud as he reached inside the truck and took out a thermos of coffee. Joe Mack didn't care to work in the heat of the day, so he'd gotten up early this day to repair the fence line on the Six Bar Ranch boundary. "This is a job for wetbacks anyway," he grumbled to himself. He would much rather have grumbled to another human being, or even his horse,

Strawberry, if either had been around. He fancied himself a cowboy and was glad to be shuck of those Marine Corps fatigues and that confusing, ugly mess in Southeast Asia. He had served alongside Ripley's Raiders. By the grace of God he had survived the Tet Offensive, and much of what he had seen and experienced he'd just as soon not bring up, and better still, have evaporate from his memory in the dry, West Texas sun. It was Nixon's problem to get the United States out of that rat hole now, and you could plainly see how much the president had aged while in office. LBJ had left office with that abysmal conflict still in process. Joe Mack didn't take much stock in the surface gloss that the media gave on politicians; he was proud of Lyndon Johnson being from Texas, although he sided with a lot of good ole boy rumor that the man was just another crook. Still, Johnson was a driving force behind the electric coops, and in this part of the country the Rio Grande Electric Coop was a big one, with the fewest customers per mile of anywhere in the United States.

Viet Nam—he wished he'd never heard of the place. He'd been proud to be a Marine, although he felt those fancy dress blues they took your picture in looked decidedly better on other men than on his lanky frame. Once they heard he was some cowboy from Texas, they made him a sniper. He had bonded with an M-14 rifle in that rank jungle for nearly eighteen months, then, good riddance. The old things they had drilled into his head came back to him in flashes, "this is my rifle, there are many like it, but this one is mine….B.R.A.S.S.—Breathe, Relax, Aim, Stop, Squeeze…when I kill the only thing I feel is recoil…Of course, that last statement was sickeningly untrue. He felt for the fate of the poor South Vietnamese who wanted a lifestyle free of tyranny like in the United States. He had recently noticed a recruiting poster in town that featured a drill instructor getting into some recruit's face, and the caption was, "We Don't Promise You A Rose Garden," which was a tongue-in-cheek reference to a Lynn Anderson country western tune by that same name, *Rose Garden*. He had witnessed a lot of horrible things, but perhaps one of the scariest was when he had been part of a squad on a reconnaissance mission one cloudy, drizzly night. They had set out some Claymore mines along what they believed to be a popular trail among the Viet Cong. A Claymore was a directional explosive triggered by a pull-string to trip it—either unknowingly by the enemy or intentionally by the

Marines who set them. It was like setting off a bunch of ball bearings with an explosion behind them—very nasty device. That night they had set out their Claymores and were waiting in the bush when the clouds started to break up just a little. To their horror, they discovered they were in close proximity to an entire VC battalion! That Claymore had to be retrieved and retrieved stealthily and fast. All six of them would be annihilated or taken prisoner should they be found up against such overwhelming odds. Mack recalled that a buddy of his, Cpl. Lopez, had volunteered to crawl out and retrieve the device; fortunately he was successful. But the ordeal wasn't over. As they lay in the bushes with hearts pounding in their throats and knots in their stomachs, a VC soldier came patrolling right up to them. Did he suspect they were there? Should they shoot and make a run for it? No—definite suicide—they must remain perfectly still and quiet. They soon learned, much to their chagrin, that the Viet Cong was coming to relieve himself just off the trail, and directly into the bushes where they lay! Neither Mack, nor any other of the survivors of that night ever forgot the acrid smell of urine as it spattered onto them through the dense leaves and branches of the bushes they were hiding in. They lived to tell the tale and to hate that ugly conflict. It was a different culture there, and Joe Mack with his simple country ways never quite grasped the tenacity or brutality of either his adversaries or his fellow Marines. Decidedly, he understood Mexicans better than Vietnamese and, frankly, some of his best friends were Mexicans—although they staunchly defended the fact that they were Texans, and that Mexicans lived on the south side of the Rio Grande not that far away. Hell, he used to play "Alamo" at school at recess during his youth; the Hispanics would be the Mexicans, and the Anglo boys the Texans who defended their values at that little Spanish mission in present-day San Antonio. Of course, according to Joe Mack, the white boys always won...

The morning, as was typical, had started off a cool one. It would get blistering hot soon enough, but for now the turkey vultures were perched on the fence posts with their wings spread out and their backs to the east catching the early rays to warm them up for a day of scavenging along Highway 62-180, which went between El Paso and Carlsbad, or down Highway 54 to Van Horn along the Sierra Diablo Mountains.

"Takes me a while to warm up myself," Joe mused aloud. He was in no hurry to get on this project—nothing much worse than fixing fence. If only a man could stay in the pickup or up on horseback—that's the kind of cowboying Joe fancied. He'd work a few hours here, then go check that crippled windmill down at the base of the Delaware Mountains.

He flipped the cigarette butt down at the base of some prickly pear cactus and crushed it out with his boot. The grass was sparse here and the dusty, rich clay soil was littered with small rock fragments. A striped whip-tail lizard skittered off into the greasewood, and Joe Mack was thankful it wasn't a rattlesnake. Had to watch out for them darn things and it behooved a man to always be able to see where he was planting his next step. Out here it was over an hour to a town of any worth, and if you happened to get bit by a Mojave you'd be dead before you got there anyway.

Two weeks ago, Joe had been driving at night down 54 toward Van Horn when he ran out of gas. "Bad habit, not having enough gas in this country," he had mused. He had started to get out of the truck and walk when he trusted his better judgment—and his very nature—not to be doing anything rash—especially afoot. Too many rattlesnakes like to come out on the warm pavement at night as the desert rapidly cools off. He didn't know if it was a *good way* to get bit, but it was definitely a way of tempting fate in this country.

Joe tugged on his greasy, ragged leather gloves and tied on a nail apron with fence staples in it. All he would need was a pair of fence pliers, a hammer, and a block and tackle to occasionally stretch some loose wire. There were a good five paces between the fence posts on this stretch, and Joe beefed up the barrier by putting a couple of thin cedar stays in between. There was a pleasant, somewhat pungent fragrance of greasewood as the landscape heated up. Some folks didn't like it, but Joe always appreciated how strong and pleasant greasewood smelled, most notably after a rain. A little rain definitely changed the dynamics in this country; you could have water running over the road or through a normally dry wash from a sudden rainstorm that had occurred up in the mountains. Rain was good, and scarce, but it brought with it certain hazards a man had to be aware of. Lightning had on occasion killed cowboys in this country—and the horses they were riding as well. Joe had several friends get struck over near the Moon Ranch, and only one rider lived to tell the tale. That man claimed the clouds weren't even directly overhead, that they appeared a little to the west of them when the bolt came crashing down. Ole Stub Rogers had some hearing loss from that episode, as well as a healthy respect for lightning evermore.

"Aw, I'll just do about another hundred feet of fence line and then go to the Delaware Well," Joe said aloud, "What do you think, Red, ready to haul me over to the base of the Delaware's?" Red was the name he had given his faded red Chevy truck; his affinity for the machine was in words only though, as witnessed by the tailgate that was wired shut, some badly dented fenders and scratched paint, and plenty enough rust where the paint had oxidized off in the intense desert sun.

Joe finished the hundred-foot section of fence, then spread out some bundles of fence staves every so far to resume work later on. Even if they lay there a year, there would be little to no rot lying on the arid desert ground.

He dug out his lunch box and rounded up a little fuel for a small cooking fire. There was not much around except for dead branches from creosote bushes and mesquite. During this forage for fuel he spied a small, mummified Texas horned lizard impaled on the thorn of a mesquite—the thorn went through its head, right through an eye. Joe had never seen anything do that, but had heard it was done by a bird, a shrike. Although it was part of nature, somehow it gave him a chill, as if it were a bad omen about something about to happen. Nevertheless, he gathered enough sticks to make a little flame as he took his Zippo lighter to the fine dry grass and twigs he had for tinder. Joe Mack had a couple of hot dogs and tortillas along and a can of pork and beans. With gloved hands and a big folding pocket knife, he cut open the top of the bean can. He well recalled an episode doing this when he was younger when he had cut the knuckle on his index finger on the jagged tin when the knife slipped through too fast. Sometimes in cold weather, he still had a little discomfort in that joint. Joe broke off a green branch from a creosote bush, whittled a clean end with his knife, and roasted the hot dogs over the fire.

While he ate, he noticed a shaggy looking coyote approaching his location from upwind. Joe Mack snuck over to the truck and grabbed his 30:30 Winchester from off the rack behind the seat. He lay on the ground, resting the barrel between the barbs on the fence wire. It wasn't exactly the precision weapon that his M14 had been in the Corps, but it was decidedly a more cowboy weapon. The unsuspecting coyote could neither smell nor hear him with the wind in Mack's favor. When he trotted into range, Mack squeezed off a shot, missing the coyote by inches, kicking up dirt under its belly. The coyote made an almost comical jump up into the air with its back arched like a miniature bronc. "Ha, ha—lucky devil," Mack commented aloud, "lucky for you I jerked the trigger. Aw, what the heck, good luck to you out there, but leave the sheep and calves alone!"

He gazed out over the landscape, toward the salt lakes, the name kind of a misnomer for an arid expanse of salt and sand that occasionally harbored a shallow sheen of water on a rare year after a heck of a lot of rain. It was hard to believe that the Permian Sea had once covered this area, and that sharks and fish and other sea creatures had flourished where he now desperately tried to scratch out a living. Blood had been spilled over the rights to the salt in the old days; a shoot-out in El Paso was referred to as the El Paso Salt Wars.

There was some occasional processing of the salt in some areas, though nothing like in the late 1800s. Joe Mack recalled reading about the El Paso Salt War of 1877 where violence erupted over the rights to mine salt here at the base of the Guadalupe's. There were factions heavily involved on both sides of the trickling border of the Rio Grande, and it escalated into a race war between the Mexicans and the gringos. It was politically as well as racially charged, and an inexperienced Texas Ranger detachment earned the dubious distinction of being the only one in history to give up its arms and surrender to an enemy. Joe Mack was no history expert, but he calculated that if the Rangers hadn't perhaps it would've been a miniature Alamo, with a few more dead heroes, and fewer survivors to embellish on the episode.

There was no telling how you would handle such situations until you were in them. Perhaps if Joe Mack had been in the green Lieutenant Tays' position, he may have slung lead and died young. Then again, he might've turned coward and found some way to run. One thing for certain, he didn't have the political ambition, ego, or devil-may-care attitude that Judge Charlie Howard had during that incident. No matter what, some critic, some day, would point out how you could've done better. Nevertheless, that coyote earlier had done better this day. He would live another day to chase rabbits or mice or seek out roadkill or hapless calves and sheep.

Mack recalled getting to ride in an airplane on one occasion for another ranch outfit, just to shoot coyotes from the air. It had seemed terribly unfair, but that's what the boss had ordered, and he was paying the bills. Besides, it was fun flying and not something Mack had done much of in his life. Nothing personal against them coyotes really, but you had to reduce predation on livestock. Actually, he loved hearing the coyotes howl out in the desert on a calm night—something simple, beautiful, and sort of romantic about it. Maybe he'd been influenced by too much Bob Wills and Marty Robbins music and paperback westerns. Naw, he knew what he liked, and he was his own man. He was a man of the West but, alas, born a few decades too late.

"Ah, this is living here, man! Simple pleasures really are the best!" He wrapped the hot dog in a tortilla, wishing he had some onion and ketchup to go on it—but this would do. That and some cold pork and beans was a pretty doggone good meal. Joe Mack fished a Zane Grey paperback Western out of the glove box of the truck. It was a dog-eared copy he'd picked up at a secondhand bookstore somewhere, but it read good. He stretched out on a bare piece of ground and took in a chapter—just to give his mind an escape into another world in a different time—for a little while.

Old Red rattled on down the trail, up onto the highway, and back onto a winding dirt ranch road. *Fortunate Son* by Creedance Clearwater Revival blared on the radio. Joe Mack definitely identified with it as the lyrics were in tune with his past:

"... Some folks inherit star-spangled eyes,
Ooh, they send you down to war, Lord,
And when you ask them, "How much should we give?"
Ooh, they only answer More! more! more! yoh,

It ain't me, it ain't me, I ain't no military son, son.
It ain't me, it ain't me; I ain't no fortunate one, one.
It ain't me, it ain't me, I ain't no fortunate one, no no no..."

At the Delaware Well he disconnected the sucker rod and used some large pipe wrenches to hoist the pipe out of the well a short section at a time. His arms were long and strong as spring steel, despite his aversion to certain types of work. He methodically installed new leathers and changed the oil in the windmill's gearbox up above.

As the black, dirty oil, warm as blood, spilled out and over his arms, Joe Mack broke out in a cold sweat. He clung to the metal framework of the windmill tower with a fixed stare in his eyes. For the moment, he was not in West Texas, but in Viet Nam in a downed helicopter with numerous casualties on board. He and a lieutenant were basically unscathed and commenced removing wounded survivors, and worse yet, body parts of others. The pilot was still strapped into his seat with the ruined aircraft tilted at an angle. Cpl. Joe Mack noted that a razor-sharp, jagged piece of metal was precariously close to the pilot's neck. Any slight shifting of the aircraft, any wrong move by the bewildered, unwary pilot would be his demise. Cpl. Mack worked his way through the gore and debris toward the pilot. Captain Williams, the pilot, mumbled a little, obviously wounded and in pain.

"Don't move, Captain Williams!" Cpl. Mack pleaded.

"Huh?" the Captain muttered, turning his head.

His very movement cut the jugular artery on his own neck and red hot spurts of blood began pumping out into the cockpit and all over Cpl. Mack's arms and face. In less than a minute, he bled out and died.

Refocusing on the present, and realizing that the hot liquid on his arms and face was crankcase oil, not blood, Joe Mack began to recover. Blurry vision that seemed as real as the West Texas sun gradually let go of the steamy, green jungle images of Viet Nam and gave way to the arid surroundings of the Chihuahuan Desert. Symbolically, several turkey vultures came into view, incessantly seeking out the demise of some other creature in their own quest for survival.

Black, dirty oil was still spilling all over the tower and ground below. Joe Mack shook his head and sat down to compose himself and collect his senses. He had experienced these episodes before; the doctor at the VA Hospital assured him that they would diminish as time passed by. Once composed, he reassessed the task at hand, which was the windmill repair. At last satisfied when it was all reassembled and pumping water in the stout Texas wind, Joe Mack sat down on the edge of a feed bunk that had salt and mineral block in it to reward himself with a cigarette. Bad habit, smoking. Damn Marine Corps had gotten him into that habit as well; it didn't help with those cute little packs of cigarettes they included in the C-rations. At first, he had given them away or traded for something edible. But eventually the stress, the peer pressure, maybe just juvenile stupidity—gave way to a nasty habit. At the time, he'd even smoked the harsher fare like Lucky Strike and Pall Malls.

Lonely country, West Texas—could be. Especially of late, Joe Mack knew and appreciated the meaning of true loneliness. His wife Cassie had left him and moved in with some rig hand from Roswell, New Mexico, just short of a year ago. It didn't work out with that guy either, and she had since called Joe wanting to make amends, wanting to give their marriage another chance. She had written a letter recently that he kept folded up in his wallet. Every now and then, he would pull it out and read it and meditate on the possibilities. Joe didn't know if he could oblige, not that he was incapable of forgiveness. He exhaled some smoke, wondering if he should give her a call, wondering if he could truly trust her again. Sure, he had friends, lots of them. Everyone liked Joe Mack. He had a quiet wit and charm not unusual in cowboys in this part of the country. He didn't always reply quickly, but he replied wisely in most situations. He supposed that if they had children involved it would be another story altogether—a lot more to factor in. Despite the hippie culture that was going on in much of the country, Joe could never abandon his own flesh and blood. He sure missed Cassie—perhaps it was in part that they hadn't as yet committed to having a family of their own that brought about the breakup—he didn't know. Sometimes, visions in his mind of her sleeping with another man and what they were doing tormented him until he had to shut off the thoughts. Thoughts of her enjoying carnal pleasures with someone else and not him. Why was he so bad, so unappealing? Yet, he did love her, and deep down he suspected that she genuinely loved him, too. Joe flipped the cigarette butt into the gypsum sand and declared in his mind that he would call her—soon—maybe today.

With a metallic bang, he tossed the paint-bare, rusty, dirty oil-soiled wrenches into the bed of the pickup. Joe washed his hands in the sand, getting the bulk of the blackened oil off of his hands.

"Must be near a hundred degrees, Red," he mused as he opened his battered metal coffee thermos to wring out one final cup. He downed the coffee and thirst not slaked took the cup to the windmill and caught some cool sparkling water coming out of the pipe. In this country, water might as well be liquid silver or gold—it was that valuable—maybe more. Up in the Guadalupes there were springs and running water, just as clear as window glass. In McKittrick Canyon, the water would flow a ways, then disappear, and reappear further downstream. It was a big deal, good clean water in this desert country.

In the days of old, the Mescalero Apache's last stronghold was in the Guadalupes. There one could find water, game, and a variety of plant food. Perhaps most notable was the century plant, or agave. Within that symmetrical cluster of spear-pointed green leaves was a sweet core that was like potatoes to the Apache. Of course, it could also be made into an alcoholic beverage, mescal, which was a pretty popular item south of the border; hence the name Mescalero Apache. Yes, the Apache knew where all the water sources were; trouble was, in time, so did the U.S. Cavalry. Colonel Benjamin H. Grierson, commander of the 10th Cavalry out of Fort Davis, to the south of the Guadalupes, made it a point to learn. Grierson was the commander an all-black regiment, save for the white officers—Buffalo Soldiers they had been called. It would probably never get mentioned in the history books, but Joe Mack learned these things from people whose roots went deep in this part of West Texas. He had, in fact, helped round up cattle near Rattlesnake Springs on the east side of the Sierra Diablos, where Apache Chief Victorio had made his last attempt on the 10th Cavalry trying to get to water at Rattlesnake Springs. The cavalry successfully repelled the attackers, and Victorio and his band retreated into Mexico where Mexican troops would eventually present him and his band with their demise.

Joe Mack fired up Old Red and headed for home—he would give Cassie a call—maybe it was worth a shot. He had only gone a few miles down the highway when the local Texas Highway Patrol officer, with his lights flashing, pulled him over. Once stopped, Trooper Jim Conklin turned off his lights.

CHAPTER 2

An Evil Wind Cometh

"What's new, Mack?" Conklin asked casually as he tipped back his Western-style straw patrol hat and as Joe looked out his driver's side window.

"Oh, not much exciting, Jim, just shorin' up a little fence, and I put some new leathers on that Delaware Well windmill."

"Got her pumpin' a good stream, Mack?"

"Yeah, pretty good. Had me a taste of it, good water. Not as good as a beer though."

"Beer?" Jim asked incredulously. "Don't you drink that rotgut Falstaff beer?"

"It's brewed in El Paso," Joe defended; they used to make a real local Texas beer, Mitchell's."

"That may be so, but they might've cleaned up that muddy Rio Grande water a little before they skipped some hops and barley across it and bottled it."

Joe Mack just grinned; he knew Conklin was a teetotaler originally from South Texas.

"So, did you just pull me over to visit or are you arresting me for something?" Joe Mack asked with grinning blue eyes.

"Arrest you? Good grief, Mack, nothing that serious. You might fix your taillights on this junk heap though, nothing's working back there. Probably ripped your wiring loose driving through all that greasewood and mesquite out there."

"Yeah, I been meaning to get that done one of these days," Mack lied.

"Well, be careful Mack. Meet me for coffee sometime up at the Pine Springs Café."

"If you're buyin', it's a date," Joe Mack promised.

Joe Mack proceeded on to his trailer house out in the middle of nowhere. He stopped at the entrance to his long, winding driveway off the highway and grabbed his mail. That infernal West Texas wind was blowing its usual annoying mischief, sucking what little moisture was anywhere near the surface of the ground and making the dust blow where the ground had been cultivated. They'd found good groundwater in what was now Dell City back in the forties and there was a lot of chilies, tomatoes, cotton, and alfalfa being grown there now and on some ground near there as well. Dell City wasn't much, but it did have a school, several churches, and nearly a dozen bars to get into trouble in.

Joe Mack parked his truck and went into the trailer. He flipped on the swamp cooler and cracked a couple of windows to try to cool off that sweltering tin-clad dwelling. He opened the fridge and looked longingly at a cold beer, then decided better of it and grabbed a Dr. Pepper instead. He fumbled for a bottle opener in one of the cluttered kitchen doors and popped the cap off the bottle of Dr. Pepper. "10-2-4" it said on it—whatever that meant. Probably that it went down tasty at most any time of the day or night. That was a good southern drink too, and it didn't cloud a man's head at all. He plopped down in the worn-out easy chair, giving the swamp cooler a chance to do its job and cool him off just a tad, while he sipped on the cold Dr. Pepper and stared at the dusty bookshelf on the wall. He stared at a photo of him and Cassie, standing by Strawberry out at the coral. He'd named him after that song by Marty Robbins, *Strawberry's Last Ride*. Dear God, they'd had some special times; Mack longed for those times and wondered if Cassie had the same yearning in her heart. In daydreaming fashion, he got up and picked up the picture to take a closer look at it. The shelves were awfully dusty, but they matched the rest of his abode. Mack stroked his index finger along the surface, exposing a shiny polyurethane finish on top of walnut stain on the woodwork. Beside the photo was a small seashell, a conk he had heard it called. What was special about it was that it didn't come from the Gulf of Mexico. This shell had come from the Permian Sea. Cassie had found it right here on his property. He reflected back to that time; he and Cassie had only been married a few months and had moved onto this place with a trailer and a couple of suitcases. Friends had assisted with a horse trailer to move their acquired furnishings, tools, and other personal effects. They had been out walking around when Cassie spotted the small, bone-white shell protruding from the sand.

"Look at this, Joe," she exclaimed in amusement. "Do you suppose this came here naturally?"

"Why shore," Joe started off with a twinkle in his eyes, "this was prime beachfront property thirty, forty years ago! Stub Rogers was a lifeguard back then!"

Cassie took her battered straw cowboy hat and playfully hit at him with it as he laughed.

"If Stub Rogers was ever seen in a pair of swim trunks his lily-white legs would cause even a pack of coyotes to stampede!" she laughed. "Let's keep it, something to remember this day by, in our first year of marriage—from our honeymoon to a 'beach resort'!"

Joe Mack smiled, reflecting back on that time, not wanting it to fade away and leave him stranded here in this miserable present. But all good daydreams have to end sometime.

With sweaty palms and a queasy stomach, he picked up the phone to call. Dead. Deader'n a doornail. Joe Mack recalled some mail from the phone company and he opened it up. His phone had been disconnected due to his being delinquent in paying his bill. Fact was, he'd been months' delinquent, and if he wasn't careful—or more prosperous—the electricity would be next. "Heck of a note," he thought, "Now I'll have to drive to the Salt Flat Café to use the pay phone." She might not be home anyway, he thought—could be at work—or worse yet, with somebody. Somehow, he didn't really believe that last part—after all, she had just recently called him. Joe set down the thick glass bottle of Dr. Pepper and headed out the door. He paused long enough to pat Strawberry on the neck and talk to him a little, to feel that velvety nose as Strawberry ate a couple of sugar cubes out of his hand. Strawberry whinnied softly and shook his head—he was glad to see his owner and best friend, Joe Mack. "Wish me luck, Strawberry," Joe said softly, "better yet, pray for me. Good Lord, what am I saying, you'd think this horse was human!" With that he hopped in Old Red and headed for the pay phone at the Salt Flat.

There were several pickup trucks outside the Salt Flat Café, one of them a newer model with "Quiones Wool Buyers" painted on the door panels. No doubt a buyer checking out the local sheepmen in this part of West Texas and Southeast New Mexico. Joe Mack fumbled with his cigarette pack and dropped the pack on the ground by the front door. He noticed when he was picking it up an odd-looking heel print in the soft dirt. It had to be from one of the customers inside because the wind and dust wouldn't let it remain unscathed for long. Roper style boots, he noted. On the right heel, there was either a defect or the man had accidentally stepped on a hot piece of metal that made the imprint of part of a square.

Between looking for booby traps in the jungle in Viet Nam and watching where you walked in the desert, Mack was accustomed to looking down. If there wasn't a rattlesnake waiting to bite you there was something else that would poke, scratch, or skewer you. He had once stepped on a lecheguilla, an agave-type plant with a sharp point. That had laid him up for the better part of a week to where all he could do was lie around and read some Luke Short and Louis L'Amour Westerns. Patches of lecheguilla were akin to a bunch of bayonets buried in the soil. The Viet Cong had made traps based on this principle, placing sharp sticks called bungy sticks in a small covered hole in the middle of a trail. They would place human feces on top of the sticks, and if a man stepped on it, he would get poisoning in his feet. Nasty business, which is why the U.S. military started putting metal plates in the soles of soldiers' combat boots.

Normally, Joe Mack would've gone inside to shoot the breeze with whoever might be in the Salt Flat Café, but on this occasion he didn't care even to encounter anyone he knew. He thought of that after he had sauntered into the place, as if he were going to order up a cup of coffee. At the counter paying his bill was a Mexican man with a nice new white shirt, fancy cowboy hat, and a big belt buckle that he probably hadn't earned in a rodeo. The man had a sinister countenance; somehow, and not knowing why, he sort of made Mack's skin crawl. Mack had a sense about people, horses, and situations. He wasn't always right, but he was a pretty quick study of human character. The stranger had a black hat with a silver hatband; apparently, he had just purchased gas outside and was in a hurry to go. He had a slight sheen of perspiration on him, even though he wasn't exactly dressed for physical labor. He had on a fancy pair of roper boots, so Mack assumed he was the man with the curious boot print.

At one of the tables was a group of men from an oil rig pulling crew based out of Hobbs, New Mexico. Mack didn't know them, but they were some big ole boys, and their skin was reddish brown and oil smeared from toiling in the hot sun at a man's job. The thought of that type of work never appealed to Joe Mack, although it paid quite well. Right now, he had other things to think about, things of the heart. Things of the heart were a private matter with him, though sometimes his emotions would leak out. Joe Mack waived at the waitress behind the counter, then turned around. He went in the phone booth outside the café and slipped in a dime and dialed. He listened through a few rings, then suddenly the sound of the phone being picked up.

"Hello?" came Cassie's soft, delicate voice. Mack felt a weird weakness in his legs, and he propped himself more stably inside that glass oven of a phone booth.

"Hello?" she inquired again—Mack seemed tongue tied.

"Hello, Cassie, it's me, Joe."

"How are you doin', Joe?" Just from that question, more yet from the tone, he could discern the heartbreak and yearning in her heart. Maybe it wasn't over with them—there was still a chance. It would take a lot of work, but then they had a lifetime ahead of them. Of course, it couldn't be possible, but he almost thought he caught the faint smell of her favorite perfume right there in the phone booth.

"Aw, just workin', just gettin' by. Sure do miss you, Cass. I was looking at that picture up on the bookshelf of you an' me an' ole Strawberry."

Silence. Now Cassie was tongue tied, or emotional. Two soft, steady hot streams of tears glided down her cheeks in the privacy of her little apartment. Joe Mack thought he heard a whispery, stifled sob—or maybe it was his.

"Cass, I been thinking about your letter—don't write me off just yet—I'm a little slow in my ways—heck, I guess I'm even a little scared."

"I understand," she reassured him, "heck, I can't blame you," she added, wiping tears from her cheeks and looking for a tissue to wipe her nose with.

"Maybe we could meet halfway some evening, in Carlsbad. Just have coffee or a picnic on the Pecos?"

"Yes, I'd like that, Joe. I'd like that very much."

More silence. Hearts were fluttering; it was a combination of heartache and new hope. Perhaps God himself was putting conviction upon them to give it another go.

"Joe?"

"Yes?"

"I, I love you, Joe." Now tears definitely were flowing down Joe Mack's cheeks. He lowered the front of his black felt hat, just in case someone he knew would see him. He didn't want anyone or anything to interrupt this moment. Desperately, he hungered to believe what she had just told him. He had many regrets in his life; no doubt there were shortcomings on his part of being a husband or a man in their marriage. He wasn't sure what else to do, and he was scared that seeming too anxious would drive her away for good.

"Joe? Joe, did you hear me?" At first he just shook his head reflexively, knowing full well she couldn't hear a nod, but gasping to communicate between his emotional shudderings.

"Yes," he whispered, "I love you too, Cass. I've always loved you—do you realize that?"

"Yes," she replied simply, "Maybe a little too late I realize it quite well. Joe, let's talk later, I've got to go to work now—but I want to meet you in Carlsbad. Could you call me tomorrow?"

"Sure," he replied, "I'll call you about this same time tomorrow. I love you, Cassie, I miss you something fierce."

"I miss you too, cowboy," she replied sweetly. He hadn't heard that pet name in a while, and it was an endearing term she knew full well meant a great deal to him, "cowboy." There was another pause, reluctance by both to hang up.

"Goodbye," she said.

"Goodbye, talk to you tomorrow," he promised.

Joe Mack hurried from the phone booth to his truck with his chin tucked down and his hat tipped low. Fortunately, he didn't see anyone, and he got in his truck and started the engine. He wiped his cheeks one last time and blew his nose in his grimy bandana. He had to get his head screwed on straight. He'd almost forgotten that the ranch foreman, Dan Elder, had wanted him to swing by Danny Flores' place and pick up a saddle that Danny had repaired. There probably wasn't a man in West Texas more knowledgeable about tack gear, or adept at repairing it, than Danny Flores. Mack had taken some of his own gear there over the years, though he hated to admit that there was anything at all pertaining to being a cowboy that he couldn't handle with his own two hands and vast reserve of knowledge.

Joe Mack drove up north of Salt Flat, then took a turn off toward the east to the Flores place. They really weren't that far from Highway 62-180, and it was pretty handy for anyone needing tack gear repaired. Mack pulled into the yard, almost not shutting off the truck when he didn't notice Flores' pickup or any other vehicle around. He glanced toward the house and noticed that only the screen door was closed, so possibly there was someone home. Perhaps Yolanda Flores, Danny's wife, was home, or their daughter Aubrey. Mack shuffled up to the house. Get this last little chore done and he would call it a day. He glanced at the ground and noticed that same odd heel print. Maybe it was from Danny's boot then, and not the stranger at the Salt Flat Café, or maybe that man was a wool buyer and had paid Danny a visit—he did raise some sheep. He was ready to prop up his feet and just think a spell at home. Joe Mack knocked on the unlatched screen door and it banged against the paint-bare door jamb.

"Hello?" he inquired. No answer. Complete silence. In the barren yard, a few chickens were pecking around in the dirt, and a couple of horses munched hay with little concern over in the corral. It occurred to Mack that something was peculiar here. Ole Flores had slipped up here from old Mexico when the story got out about all the good irrigation water in the Dell City area—the Valley of Hidden Waters they had called it. There had been, in fact, a nice story in the December 11, 1950, edition of *LIFE* magazine about how three Texas investors had sunk five deep wells in 1946 and found abundant water of good quality. In 1950, many of the town's residents had lived in tents and didn't even have electricity unless they had their own little power plants. Danny Flores had lived south of the border down Presidio way and had come here for better fortune back in those early days. But Flores was a cautious man, and Mack always noted that he kept his doors locked if he wasn't at home. It was a little unlike most folks in this part of the country, but maybe ole Flores had acquired that habit in his native Mexico.

Mack knocked again, and again called out, "Hello?" Suddenly, a sickening feeling filled his stomach and leadened his legs—it was an intuitive dread of discovery, much like he had on occasions in Viet Nam. Mack had known this family for more than twenty years; he stepped inside the door of the little two-bedroom, cinder-block, stucco-coated home. It didn't feel right—something was wrong. Mack looked toward a bedroom doors that was open, and it was then that he saw them. Two tennis shoe-clad feet, upright and motionless at the foot of the bed. They were petite feet, those of young Aubrey. With an inner dread, Mack dredged up an inquisitive, "Aubrey? Are you okay?" No answer.

For a moment, Mack remained still. Perhaps she was just asleep. Maybe she was sick, and he should just turn around and go. But better judgment told him that Yolanda Flores would never leave her daughter home alone if she was sick. The other problem was that this wasn't the time of day for a sixteen-year-old girl to be sleeping. Mack stepped cautiously through her bedroom door. He now noticed that her blue jeans were bunched down to her ankles and there was no movement. Suddenly, it was as if a demon from hell had been waiting for this very moment—to point at Mack and laugh at him—jubilant over something insidious and cruel. Aubrey Flores lay nude on the bed, her hip area slightly covered by a sheet as if it had been tossed there with a backhand. Her eyes were wide open but glazed, and there were multi-colored bruises around her throat, indicating that a crushing grip by powerful hands had robbed this little girl's virtue, her chance of being a wife and mother, and her life itself. She seemed too pale for a Mexican girl, and Mack looked quickly away after his initial shock. Had it not been for the atrocities he had seen in Nam, he might've vomited on the spot. She had been such a sweet, lovely girl—a true gentle spirit.

"Oh, dear God!" he exclaimed aloud. Who would do such a horrid thing? Resorting to his combat training, he shook her and asked if she was okay. But he knew better. He checked for a pulse anyway, and there was none. Already her body was a little cooler than it should've been, but she wasn't stiff. This hadn't happened very long ago! Mack attempted to close her eyelids, but when it didn't go easy on the first try he felt repulsed and sick inside. Mack looked frantically around the room—for what he didn't know. There was a discernible ringing in his ears, and his hands became clammy. How he wished this was just a nightmare that he could wake up from. Part of him wished he could give up his life for poor Aubrey, but those arrangements simply weren't possible. He went to the kitchen and picked up the phone to call Jim Conklin. The phone, like poor Aubrey, was dead. Mack was suffocating in sympathy for the parents of this poor girl, and for poor Aubrey herself. He wanted no part of this pain and suffering, he had enough of his own to bear already. Frantic, he knew he must go back to Salt Flat and get to a phone. Mack hustled to his truck and spun out of the driveway to get some law enforcement there fast. As he was nearing the road, a truck with two Mexican men was slowing down to turn into the Flores place. Mack had his window down and somewhat incoherently tried to convey to them that something dreadful had happened at the Flores place. "Como?" they inquired with confused looks on their faces, obviously not understanding a word of English.

In frustration, fear, and dread, Mack sped off toward Salt Flat to get hold of some law enforcement. It occurred to him slightly after he left the men that the Spanish-speaking strangers might end up being detrimental witnesses as to his association with the crime scene. "Man, that was stupid, Joe!" he cursed aloud at himself.

CHAPTER 3

Shoot—out at Salt Flat

In a rare state of panic, Joe Mack barged into the Salt Flat Café and blurted out that something terrible had happened just up the road at the Flores place. He gave a shotgun delivery of what he knew and ordered the waitress to call the police. Mack had to get to Dell City, try to get in touch with Danny and Yolanda Flores before anyone else to break the tragic news to them. Maybe he could find the sheriff there as well.

As he raced up Highway 62-180 toward the Dell City exit, Joe Mack's mind was racing. He had just left a crime scene. There was some poor little girl back there who had this very day—probably while he repaired the Delaware mill—been raped and murdered. He was no doubt the first person on the scene after the killer, and he had left that scene with two unknown witnesses he tried to talk to—who could identify him. His fingerprints would be all over that house—on the screen door handle, on the telephone!

Dang it! He should've tried to call Conklin himself, although he likely wouldn't have gotten hold of him personally. It was unfair to dump such a burden on the elderly waitress at the Salt Flat Café, but his mind wasn't thinking clearly. Perhaps, even Trooper Conklin wouldn't believe his story.

Mack pulled off the side of the road and tried to collect his thoughts. Old Red's engine just idled as he pondered what to do next. Should he try to find Danny and Yolanda? Even inquiring, it would be hard not to leak word of the tragedy that had just occurred.

Perhaps, he should return to the home and wait for law enforcement or go back to the Salt Flat Café and learn what they had found out. He would have to give a statement to the police. It dawned on him that he—Joe Mack—would be a prime suspect.

Joe Mack turned around on the highway, not sure where to go or who to contact next. He would go back to the Flores crime scene. Before he turned off the highway, he could see flashing lights in the distance at the Flores place. Dear Lord, how quickly law enforcement had arrived—the waitress at the Salt Flat Café must've been operating with a clearer head than he had been. Then a thought occurred to him again. The waitress! Might'nt she think he looked rattled and strange when he came into the café? He didn't know the lady, but he heard her husband worked at the gas camp by the Patterson Hills.

Joe Mack was smart enough to know that things potentially weren't looking at all good for him. And that dimwit Hudspeth County sheriff would be looking for a simple solution to a heinous crime—and fast. Obviously, it was done by some traveler on the highway; this was no crime of passion. It had been a spontaneous act of lust and violence when the assailant happened upon an opportune situation. Likely, whoever it was didn't pull up to the Flores place with any such thing in mind.

Never matter, though, Joe Mack had the sinking feeling that he would soon be the suspect, and with all the negative things that were said about Viet Nam vets these days, he would be a prime suspect. Baby killers, murderers, war mongers—that's what a lot of the picket signs said. He would be immediately labeled as some deranged ex-Marine, and "once a Marine, always a Marine," the saying goes. Some hippie had spit in his face as he walked through the airport in his uniform in Los Angeles. It was one of the hardest things he had ever done—not to hit that punk. Mack had no use for hippies, the ugly brutality one witnesses in war, or crooked politicians. He didn't particularly want to get drawn into what many described as Exxon's War either, but he was the lucky winner of the wrong draft number for an all-expenses-paid trip to Southeast Asia. Even so, he anguished over the demise of the South Vietnamese people who so valiantly fought to rid themselves from the evil tide of communism. He reflected how tragic it was that all the human sacrifice, heroics, and suffering would be for naught, as it appeared his beloved country was, in the end, going to sell out the desperate South Vietnamese to their northern aggressors.

He just wanted to live a simple life; he just wanted to be a cowboy, riding the range, checking the stock. He loved roping competitions at little places like the Dell City Fair—even though he had lost part of his index finger during one of those outings. He missed that digit from time to time, but it was a common injury to calf ropers. In some respects, it was sort of a macho badge of honor among the breed of people he cottoned to.

Perhaps too impulsive in his thinking, Mack turned toward his place. Too late! Flashing lights were coming up behind him, and it wasn't Jim Conklin's patrol car. A mature trooper like Conklin would prevail with a level of calm and factor in what he knew about Joe Mack. That couldn't be said for whoever was pulling him over now. Mack shifted into flight or fight mode. Survival, fear, panic—everything was going south fast. He recalled he had the 30:30 Winchester on the rifle rack and at least a box or two of shells. In the glove box was an old .38 revolver wrapped in rag that a buddy had given him as payment for some work he couldn't afford to pay for. It didn't even have a holster, and more likely than not the box of bullets for it was about empty. No matter—he fished the revolver from the glove box and emptied the box of cartridges into his hand and put them in his pocket. He sped off down the highway, disregarding the squad car's flashing lights and blaring siren. It was embarrassing and scary all at the same time to Mack. He grew up in this country, he knew most everyone around. Now he was wrongly being made a spectacle of for something horrible that he hadn't done.

Up in the distance, to the east, a couple of squad cars were approaching from adjoining Culberson County, lights flashing. How could things get any worse? In desperation, Joe Mack whipped off the highway headed for a barely noticeable vehicle trail through ranch land, headed toward the salt lakes. Perhaps there was some strange curse associated with the glaring white, flat as a bread board, terrain which to him, was pretty much worthless country except in intrinsic value.

Old Red flew up over a rise, going airborne for a short distance, then slamming down hard. Junk from the truck seat went flying into the dash, and tools slammed into the front of the truck bed just behind his seat. His pursuer slowed down and kept to the highway, smart enough to know that a car wasn't going to traverse the terrain very well. Besides, there was a better road if they knew about it that went back into to the same area. They could cut him off if they were smart enough. The sun would be down in an hour or two, and then they could all deal with the challenge of darkness.

Mack kept racing along, far faster than he knew was wise, on an old cow path that he had at best been on once or twice years ago. Suddenly, he hit a washout that caused the ball joint to give way on the passenger side, disabling him on the west side of the salt lake. To his horror, several squad cars were making their way up the east side, lights and sirens going. They would be on him momentarily, easily able to drive on the dry, flat salt bed, as there had been no rain in a long, long time. A war had been fought over this salt in the old days of the El Paso Salt War; perhaps there would be another war. Mack stuffed the .38 in his pants with the pistol grip sticking out at his belt line and grabbed the 30:30 and whatever shells he could find on the floor of the truck. He took off running like a crazy man. Immediately, he could hear a man on a megaphone and thought maybe the voice was that of Jim Conklin. The message blurted wasn't halt, but, "Hey man, where the hell do you think you're going?" "Had to be Conklin to come up with a line like that at a time like this," Joe mused to himself. He knew there was little to nowhere to go, and besides, there were snakes out there. Joe Mack headed back for the truck, at least there was some level of cover there, and besides, his pursuers would be looking into the sunset.

He made a running jump to the side of the truck when he stumbled, discharging a shot from the rifle. Shouldn't've had it cocked! Damn! Now the fight was on.

Jim Conklin couldn't believe that Joe Mack would fire a shot at law enforcement—despite the allegations. Granted, he had come up on something ugly and tragic and was the only live body anyone could hang it on at present. Still, Jim knew this man; he couldn't do such a thing. He suspected that had Joe and Cassie had a daughter of their own, they would want her to be just like Aubrey Flores. Not much chance of that now and some of his colleagues were some inbred white trash with big egos and shit for brains hiding behind a badge.

"He's shooting at us!" Deputy Slaughter hollered, anxious to retaliate a hundred fold.

"Don't get hasty, boys," Conklin cautioned, "That might've just been to get our attention for a talk."

"Well, he sure as hell got our attention," Slaughter shouted red faced, snatching a shotgun with double-aught buckshot from his sedan.

They had indeed driven up on the salt lake and weren't more than sixty or seventy yards away from Joe Mack's disabled truck. Impulsively, recklessly, Deputy Slaughter ran up about ten yards and cut loose, jacking several shells through the pump shotgun. Like ball bearings, the buckshot filled the side of Joe Mack's truck with holes. Somehow the sound of the shot punching through the metal of his truck door and the side of Old Red almost made Joe sick. Sure, the old truck was a bit beat up, but they might as well have been shooting his horse. But the more sobering reality was that they were trying to shoot *him!* Guilty until proven innocent, was that the deal? Or until dead...

"Knock it off, you darn fool—I'm running this show!" Conklin shouted in rage, running after the headstrong deputy.

In response, Joe Mack, unscathed, spent a round from his Winchester that ricocheted off the salt lake near the feet of Slaughter.

"Get back there before you get shot!" Conklin shouted, grabbing Slaughter by the shirtsleeve. "I know this kid, he didn't rape and murder that Flores girl, and I'm sure I can prove it!" But as they hustled back to the other members of the posse, another shot snapped off, this time hitting Conklin in the back of his thigh. He went down with a shout, nearly taking Slaughter to the ground with him.

Even in the vanishing light and blowing dirt, you could quickly see blood soaking through Conklin's trousers. The bullet had missed the bone, but it was a bad wound that required immediate medical attention, one that would put him out of commission for a while.

"Shoot him, you idiots!" Deputy Slaughter shouted as he grabbed Conklin under the armpits and pulled him to relative safety behind a squad car.

"Just hold on a minute, fellas," Kenny Jones countered; he was the Hudspeth County sheriff and Slaughter's supervisor. "We've got to get Conklin treated and out of here to a hospital, you want him to bleed to death? Darn fool," he muttered the last for Slaughter's benefit. Neither of them was a prize, but Jones at least had a less volatile temper.

Jones ripped the back of the trouser leg open; Conklin was grimacing in pain and moaning. A posse member grabbed a first-aid kit and they applied a pressure dressing to the wound. Jones had Slaughter call in for an ambulance, preferably from Van Horn since it had a hospital; otherwise, he would have to go to Carlsbad. This operation wasn't going well at all at this point, Jones mused, out here on the salt flats in a dust storm, the sun setting, a fugitive on the run, and an officer down. And doggone it, he knew Joe Mack too—knew he was a cowboy who could shoot straight, had a lot of friends, and knew the country around here better than most. Besides, he was an ex-Marine and Viet Nam veteran—he could revert to a killer instinct. Maybe he had already flipped his lid, maybe something made Joe Mack snap inside. Everyone knew he had been torn up over his wife leaving him a year ago…

Joe Mack saw that an officer was down, but the wrong one. He meant to wound the knucklehead who tried to blow him to pieces with that scattergun in retaliation for an accidental discharge that didn't hurt anyone. No matter now, he had to get them on the defensive and put some things in his favor. Mack lined up his sights on the leading squad car and flattened the two tires exposed to him. They would have one spare, but not two in that car; besides, they now had a wounded man to deal with. Mack aimed at the hood of another car. In the diminishing light he thought it might be Conklin's patrol vehicle—no matter. He shot several rounds through the front fender into the engine area, thinking he could disable the vehicle mechanically. He was right; his random shots punctured a radiator hose, destroyed the distributor, and lodged another slug in the carburetor. Of course,

Joe Mack couldn't know the damage, but he hoped he had done enough damage to disable the vehicle somehow.

The posse retaliated by firing back a volley of pistol shots, pretty much a waste, but their sidearms were handy, and they meant to let him know they meant business. Mack crawled off about thirty feet away and hid behind a large soap tree yucca that was perched on a protruding clump of ground. Soap tree yuccas could get quite large if they lived long enough, and this one on a mound of soil at the edge of the flats was spectacular. It was twelve to fifteen feet in height with bristly arms clutching at the West Texas sky like an ominous, headless monster. For this part of the country, it was the counterpart of the Joshua tree in Southern California in appearance. Had this just been a normal day, Joe would have looked upon the ancient survivor with more reverence and appreciation. For now, it was nothing more than good cover a little ways away from Old Red. He knew his truck was their focal point, and better Old Red than himself; he'd have to start skirting off on another course out of their sight. The posse continued firing into Old Red, and now one of them apparently had a rifle.

"Darn fools can't even see what they're shooting at," Mack muttered. His head was clearing a little now; the present shoot-out that threatened his life overshadowed the horrible discovery earlier in the day. Now Mack could think tactically. He would lead these boys on a wild goose chase, then try to double back into more favorable country. He slouched low and started sneaking off to the northwest, which would take him through some sand dunes and, basically, on a path toward Dell City, or maybe beyond to Crow Flats. Of course, either destination would be stupid. Dell City only had a few hundred people, and every structure would be checked out there. And Crow Flats beyond, why, it was flat as a pancake and barren as a bread board. Without water, food, and shelter, a man wasn't going to last long in that direction. In the open country, they would simply use a search plane and set up a grid search for the posse on the ground. Initially, Mack made no attempt to hide his tracks; in fact, he tried to make sure that there were visible tracks available to his pursuers. There probably wasn't a man among them who possessed such a skill, but eventually they would have a man on it.

The posse held up fire after a fashion, pretty sure that they had at least wounded the fugitive, if they hadn't killed him. Occasionally, they fired a round or two into side of the pickup, just in case Joe Mack was alive and had the notion to slip away. They flipped on a spotlight now, but it offered limited visibility with dirt blowing in the wind. An ambulance siren was wailing in the distance, its lights flashing. Soon, Conklin would be loaded onto a gurney and hauled off to a hospital. They moved the spotlight around the area of the pickup truck. No signs of movement.

In agony, Trooper Conklin was still able to think about the situation. There was a good chance these darn fools had killed Joe Mack while the real killer was making distance. None of it did the Flores family any good. Now there might be another innocent victim lying over there on the edge of the salt flats, and damn it, now he had to go to the hospital. It was just a plain bad deal all the way around. Still, maybe Mack had eluded them.

"Now doggone it, you fools," Conklin started talking with a strain, "Quit wasting ammo and just keep the lights on that truck for a bit. Just, just, uh…" then he slipped off into unconsciousness.

"Prop his feet up, he could be going into shock!" Sheriff Jones ordered. It would be a hell of a note to have him die of shock just before the ambulance pulled onto the scene. This night definitely wasn't going smoothly, and it was dark now, and they had two disabled vehicles and a fugitive either pinned down or on the run.

CHAPTER 4

The Fugitive

Joe Mack doubled back in the night with a branch of greasewood in his hand to try to scrub out evidence of his change of direction. If the wind kept up, it would help as well by blowing dust and sand over his trail. Mack was taking a gamble on going to his trailer and getting a few supplies. Hopefully, they wouldn't think of him going there at this moment, although they would surely be there eventually. Perhaps they already had been. No matter, he would approach with caution. If he could saddle up Strawberry, he could at least make some respectable distance and buy himself some time. At this point, he was running when he could; he had to get away from the salt flats, sneak across the highway to his place, and get some supplies. His lungs were burning and his heart pounding like a hummingbird's. He wished he was in better condition, like he had been when he got out of boot camp.

The posse kept the search lights on the scene, two lights now. There was no movement, no sound. The bad thing was that if Mack was lying by that truck waiting, they had to cross a wide open piece of ground to get to him, unless they swung far around. Jones hollered out, "Joe Mack—can you hear me? Are you still alive, boy? Mack. Mack, if you can hear me bang on that truck with something!"

Nothing. No sound, no movement. The men in this posse were starting to get tired, the adrenaline had worn off now, and it was nighttime. Most would rather be at home sipping on an iced tea watching TV.

"Mack, we're coming up there in force. There's no getting away. We'll hold our fire unless you get up and run or fire a shot at us.

Don't shoot—if you do we'll all be on you and you won't stand a chance!"

As there was no response, the members of the posse just kept their eyes fixed on the scene, no one moved. After an uncomfortably long pause, Sheriff Jones directed them to spread out and approach the vehicle with caution. Soon they were upon the riddled truck scanning all about with their flashlights. Deputy Slaughter noticed footprints going toward a large soap tree yucca, and they all swung around in a crouched position looking toward that raised piece of ground and the yucca. Once they were confident that Joe Mack wasn't lying there in ambush for them, they proceeded with caution. Slaughter was taking on a new sense of purpose; he was proud of himself for finding the boot prints and getting on to the trail. So, Joe Mack had survived, and there was no blood trail. That meant the chase was still on. Slaughter soon discovered tracks leading off to the northwest.

The other members of the posse stood their ground and let Slaughter do his work. They didn't want to mess up the trail, so they waited for him to decipher the clues. Slaughter looked pensive, rubbing his square jaw with his hand. He took off his hat and wiped his sweaty brow. Then he stated with absolute conviction, "He's headed toward the sand dunes, and likely on to Dell City! A couple of us need to keep on his trail here in case he decides to double back, but we need to get patrols on those roads in the area and contact all the ranches and farms in the area to be on the lookout—subject is armed and dangerous and made an assault on a law officer!"

Joe Mack slinked across the highway and kept to the brush as he approached his trailer. He rested for a while outside the corral, looking carefully to be sure no one was waiting for him, having anticipated this possibility. Strawberry whinnied softly and came up to the fence to see him.

"Strawberry, old friend, we're going to take a ride, buddy," he spoke softly. He gently caressed the velvety soft nose, and Strawberry through habit was lipping Joe's hand, assuming he had some sort of treat, sugar cubes maybe, or a carrot or apple. Joe looked about with a pensive, worried expression etched on his brow. There was no need to hide his tracks here; they would either show up at any moment and it would be over or they would get here later and figure out what he had done.

Joe Mack saddled up Strawberry and bridled him. He tied on a partial bag of oats then led him up to the steps of the trailer and tied the bridle reins to the railing. He couldn't tarry long on this project; all too soon they would discover he'd led them off in the wrong direction.

Inside the trailer he grabbed a flashlight to keep his presence here as minimally noticeable as possible. He flung a pile of debris off the old cedar chest in the bedroom and grabbed out an old canvas pack, souvenir from the Marine Corps. Still in it was an assortment of items that could come in handy for an occasion such as this; he really didn't need to inventory it. He knew there was a first-aid kit, a poncho and poncho liner, some small throw-away can openers, "John Waynes" they had called them, and an extra set of camouflage fatigues, underwear, and socks. He knew there was a shaving kit with various items, a mirror, and a compass. The flashlight beam shown on his old jungle boots and a cartridge belt with two canteens. He didn't know why he had shipped those items home at the time, but it was looking like they might come in awfully handy now. He snatched up a hat, or "cover" as they called it in the Marines, and went out to the kitchen.

There was no time to be meticulous in what he grabbed; he simply filled his canteens with water and threw in some things from the refrigerator and cupboard that might come in handy. No concern about spoilage; he grabbed fast and furious and threw items into a plastic bag. Cans of beans, some tortillas, lunch meat, bread, several cans of sardines, tuna, and some raisins.

Swiftly, Mack packed the items onto Strawberry, made a quick drag out of some brush and a piece of rope, mounted up, then headed right up his driveway toward the highway. Mack knew of a dry wash about a hundred yards up that was pretty rocky; he exited into it off the ranch road and proceeded onward. At some point, he would have to cross Highway 54 and Highway 62-180, but he would deal with that as the time arose. He must get up into the Guadalupes where he had a chance of evading his pursuers for a while. Perhaps this would provide Conklin or some other competent law officer with integrity to find out the truth.

By now it was nearly midnight, and Joe Mack scanned the landscape for headlights before crossing over Highway 54 toward the Delaware Mountains. The Delawares looked more like big foothills, but the terrain was deceivingly rugged to the casual passerby on the highways. Mack's mind was moving fast now, strategizing, planning, and trying to keep a jump or two ahead. He would get onto the old section of Highway 62-180 that had been bypassed with the new route, thus keeping under more cover at least for a short stretch on a smooth paved surface that would also leave no trail.

It was a steep ride up a route he had remembered in the Delawares, and for a ways he went afoot, feeling safer that way due to the steep incline. Strawberry strained at the steep grade, dislodging some dirt and rocks as he scrambled to keep his footing. Despite the night chill, Strawberry was sweaty, and Joe could smell that familiar aroma of horse sweat and leather. Ah, the creaking of the saddle leather, normally a wonderful sound. Right now, any extra noise at all was disconcerting to Joe. Strawberry paused a moment and lifted his tail long enough to drop a few green horse apples. The firm round balls of dung steamed in the chill desert air. When you've got to go, you've got to go. Of all the things that had gone wrong this night, finally at least the wind had abated, and a quarter moon was giving him some light.

"I can't believe this is happening to me," Joe Mack muttered aloud, totally unafraid of anyone being in earshot out in this country. "Now I've assaulted a law officer with a weapon and resisted arrest. It's not looking good for ole Joe Mack, Strawberry, not looking good at all."

Dell City was being canvassed by an assortment of law enforcement officials and sheriff's posse members. Sheriff Kenny Jones was fast becoming doubtful that Joe Mack would really come to town seeking refuge—not a good place to hide. And to the north a ways, Crow Flats would be a suicide stretch of hell to be caught in during broad daylight—wide open, flat, very little cover, and no water. Unless, of course, that's what Joe Mack was counting on. Perhaps doing something illogical was best. If he could make it up into New Mexico....

Joe Mack paused near the old highway bridge and dismounted. It was like a ghost highway, no longer traveled, this short little by-pass stretch. Mack wondered if anyone had ever been involved in a fatal car crash here—it was certainly possible. Not that he believed in ghosts and such, but it was just an eerie feeling passing here. One poor soul he knew for sure lay in rest down in the dry wash, and that was Jose Maria Palancio. Palancio was a Mexican guide for the cavalry, and specifically for Captain Longstreet, who would rise to fame in the Confederacy during the Civil War some years later. Palancio had been ambushed and killed right in this drainage in view of the massive limestone edifice, El Capitan. El Capitan was connected to Guadalupe Peak, the highest mountain in Texas at over 8,000 feet. In this part of the world, El Capitan had been a landmark for travelers for quite some time and was certainly as prominent and recognizable in Texas as Chimney Rock was to the pioneers in Nebraska. The massive limestone edifice was the end of the line for the southern end of the Guadalupes, which continued on up into Southeast New Mexico. With a sheer drop of several thousand feet, it made for a dramatic site rising above the salt flats, with an even higher Guadalupe Peak towering over it to the north. Guadalupe Peak was the highest point in Texas at well over 8,000 feet. The Guadalupes were truly God's country.

Joe Mack reached for the cigarette pack in his pocket, then thought better of it. Not smart to risk anyone seeing the flash of his Zippo lighter or the glow of a cigarette. He drifted for a moment, thinking about the fierce Apache who held out in this region for the duration of the Indian Wars in Texas. Poor ole Palancio had been killed and then buried in a buffalo robe by the cavalry while they pursued his killers. Later, they returned to find his body had been dug up, the robe stolen from him, and more arrows shot into his dead body. "That's what you call overkill," Mack muttered softly with a chuckle, as if he were trying to amuse a friend with his wit. The wash was strewn with huge boulders and littered with prickly pear cactus, creosote bushes (greasewood, some called it), some occasional mesquite, and dwarfed desert willow.

Mack mounted up then started across the abandoned concrete bridge that still had a brass marker embedded in the concrete denoting when it was placed there by the Texas Highway Department. With the wind calmer, the sound of Strawberry's metal shoes clattered quite audibly on the concrete bridge. It was a scene reminiscent of an earlier era, a lone cowboy riding in the Guadalupes on a moonlit night, only in this case, not on the dodge from the Apache, but from law enforcement acting on a hunch.

Joe Mack listened for traffic before he proceeded closer to the highway. At this hour, it could be pretty quiet, although truckers operated through the pass at almost any hour. Joe Mack heard one approaching and pulled Strawberry up by some bushes and dismounted. He tugged on the bridle and commanded Strawberry to lie down; his loyal transport complied. The trucker flipped on his jake brake, which made kind of a low-tone machine gun sound as the compression brakes slowed the truck. The air brakes barked a little as well as he grabbed a lower gear. Just around the curve would be one more steep stretch, and then the trucker would be home free.

Joe Mack reflected on what a dangerous stretch of road this was going through Guadalupe Pass. Wind gusts in the springtime could commonly exceed a hundred miles per hour, and sustained winds of fifty to sixty miles an hour could go for days on end. It was one reason the scrub oaks didn't get very tall and also why semi-trucks and straight trucks alike would occasionally blow over. The big danger was driving through a cut in the rock; the wind would radically change directions both when you entered the cut and again when you got through it. Even being prepared, Joe Mack had been blown into the oncoming lane a time or two. At any rate, the truck had passed now, and Joe Mack couldn't hear any more coming.

"Let's go, Strawberry, get up," he said softly lifting gently on the reins. Strawberry got to his feet and Joe Mack hooked his foot in the stirrup and climbed aboard. He jumped him over a wire gate just off the highway, then crossed over and did it again on the other side. He rode up to the old rest area, looking down on the landscape below. Far off in the distance there were tiny twinklings of lights from a ranch or farm. Joe Mack dismounted, tied Strawberry to a post on a shade shelter, and then sat on the derelict picnic table. He faced away from the highway, toward Guadalupe Peak, and lit up a cigarette.

"Not much chance of anyone noticing a glow in this location," he thought to himself. He heaved in a lungful of the polluted air and then exhaled it slowly, meditating on his next move. The raisin-like smell of the tobacco was pleasant to him, and when he smoked it, it seemed to calm his nerves. Nevertheless, a bad habit that he needed to get shuck of, and it didn't do much for his wind when he was running afoot.

Joe Mack pondered for some time what to do next but finally decided he'd best get to Guadalupe Springs where there was water and even the remains of a crude shelter. He could picket Strawberry down in the chokecherry bushes and try to get a few winks before he made his next move.

By the moonlight, he proceeded on to Guadalupe Springs to the west of the old highway rest area. Ironically, he was traversing over the old Butterfield Stage road as well. At one point along the old highway was a shrine to Our Lady of Guadalupe; the Hispanic Catholics in this part of the country would come there and offer up little gifts and prayers. There were statues of Mary, coins, plastic flowers, and other artifacts left along the old highway stone guardrail, up in an alligator juniper tree. Despite the gravity of his situation, he reflected on the rich history of the mountains he was traversing. Palancio's grave was just below the rest area he had left; were it daylight, you could have spotted his stone marker to the south of the new highway. To the east, not that far away, a black trooper, Corporal Ross, had single-handedly charged at Apaches who were charging him while on a reconnaissance. Joe Mack figured it had been somewhere around Tea Kettle Hill, just west of Pine Springs.

Strawberry plodded along nonchalantly in the moonlight, picking out his steps with occasional promptings from Joe Mack on the reigns or a gentle prod with the stirrup on one side or the other near his flanks.

At Guadalupe Springs, Joe camped beside a huge old alligator juniper tree, using the flat open roof enclosure of what had once been a dugout. Strawberry was picketed a little further away. He wished so desperately that his circumstances were different, that he was camping here on this very spot, on this very night with his lovely young bride. Perhaps someday.

The massive limestone monolith of El Capitan loomed enormous behind him. Up on that impressive edifice was a mysterious, lone figure, who appeared much like the Apache of old. With a sense of vision and hearing akin more to a hawk or deer than a human, the stranger peered down at the barely discernible images of man and horse below. Neither realized that they would glimpse each other at a later point in time in these mountains and that somehow there would be a profound connection.

"How on earth will I ever be able to make a phone call to Cassie tomorrow?" Joe Mack wondered. She'd be waiting; he had promised to call. Now, he was on the run, hiding out in the mountains. By tomorrow, he would surely be on the news as well. It would be a long restless time until morning.

CHAPTER 5

Another Breed *of* Lawman

Percival Pinkerton-Whitmore looked over the case file on his desk as his cup of straight black coffee continued on its path to tepidity. "Percy," as his friends called him, was a dyed-in-the-wool Texas Ranger; he lived and breathed the life, perhaps even the myths. He had some ancestry in this business that he was at best reluctant to divulge. In some distant fashion on his mother's side, he had a relationship to a member of the Ranger detachment that had given up its arms in surrender during the El Paso Salt War. Even though it may have been the best that any man could've done in the situation, it was a piece of history Percy elected to leave out for anyone in his audience. It's possible he slipped up one time after one too many rounds of Cutty Sark and water. It was soon after that episode that Percy Whitmore battled his demons and traded the blended Scotch whiskey for ice tea, with nothing more than a slice of lemon if he had his druthers.

Now he was looking over information on a fugitive on the run in West Texas—his home territory—some ex-Marine who shot a law enforcement officer who was in the process of trying to apprehend him for questioning. Joe Mack, ranch hand, honorable service in Viet Nam, assigned to Charlie Company, military occupational skill—sniper.

Whitmore took a sip of the tepid coffee while he read on, then suddenly gave the cup a disapproving scowl as if it should've somehow known better than to have had the temerity to give up its heat in this air conditioned office environment. After a pause, Percy reluctantly gulped down the coffee anyway—no discreet way to spit it out here in the office.

This Joe Mack, this West Texas cowboy suspected of rape, murder, assault on a law enforcement officer—he could be bad news. He'd slipped the noose at the salt flats against a respectable show of law enforcement. Worse yet, Whitmore learned, this kid knew the country around there. Mack was no Johnny-come-lately; he knew that country like the back of his hand, and there were several rugged mountain ranges he could vanish into to get completely got off the radar screen.

Whitmore rubbed his brow in fatigue and stared out the office window blankly for a while. With a grunt, he got up to get a cup of hot coffee in an attempt to erase his earlier recollection of an encounter with a cold cup. Percy was starch and polish all the way. He wore black ostrich-leather roper boots, polished to a high sheen. His blue jeans were starched and ironed with a crease so sharp that you could likely shave with it. His neat salt-and-pepper hair and mustache were immaculately trimmed, with his solid jawline otherwise neatly shaved and rubbed down perhaps too liberally with Old Spice aftershave. He had a typical white, Western shirt with rhinestone snap buttons, equally as starched and creased as his blue jeans. On the road, he wore a buff-colored Stetson hat and a gray sport coat with a Western cut if the air was cool.

Percival Pinkerton Whitmore was, many claimed, a different breed of lawman. He had no particular political aspirations; unlike many, he was not on the road to dodge violence and danger in exchange for a salaried position which was relatively safe. The trouble with those bureaucratic positions, Percy speculated, was that a man was more likely to die of high blood pressure, a heart attack, ulcers, or bleeding piles. Percy had no such aspirations; he'd reached the appropriate rung on the proverbial career ladder, and he aimed to cling to it as long as his health, his wits, his nerve, and the Good Lord would allow.

Still, Whitmore was a bit of a maverick; he liked to work alone, didn't always like to stick to proper protocol. He was patient only when it was glaringly apparent that it was to his advantage to be so; otherwise, he battled his impulses on occasion and gut-level instinct almost religiously.

Certain facts raised suspicion in Percy Whitmore's objective, analytical mind on this Joe Mack case. Some of the facts could swing either way in argument to his guilt or innocence. Unless he was some West Texas, inbred, degenerate fool, it didn't make sense that the man would rape and murder the teenaged daughter of a friend of his. And a private investigator of somewhat dubious reputation in Roswell had reported to Percy that Mack and his estranged wife had been making strides toward restoring their relationship. Percy Whitmore admired that fact, if indeed it were true. He would find out firsthand, of course, since he was being assigned responsibility for spearheading this manhunt and investigation.

Whitmore had hung on to his marriage, though there had certainly been trials and tribulations. His aging wife was a chronic alcoholic who pretty much lived for cigarettes, booze, and soap operas on their little ranchette on the outskirts of El Paso. Helen Whitmore had come from a family of modest affluence and, with this in mind, they had managed a somewhat comfortable life-style in creature comforts at any rate. They had been able to have a son years ago and had raised him with great pride into his teens. Like many in these parts, he had a yearning for the ways of old, but was a good young man, lean and dark-haired like his mother and father. He was reasonably smart in school, respectful to seniors, and a pretty good hand on the pitcher's mound during baseball season. But that was before the car wreck, and Helen had been driving that night—intoxicated as was common, but less intoxicated than most of the time after the funeral.

Percy Whitmore hated what was going on in this country. He hated the whole hippie movement, drugs, sex, and rock and roll, burning flags and bras, blaspheming God, and tearing apart what had taken nearly two hundred years to build. Right down the toilet, that's where this country was headed if more level heads didn't prevail.

Putting his feet up on top of the metal desk, Percy picked up reports and attempted to read between the lines. Of course, there was always more to the story, and there were usually a few credible versions that a man on the trail wasn't privy to initially. Percy Pinkerton-Whitmore would ferret out this hombre and find out what his version of the truth was. Sure, Joe Mack might be savvy, and off with a small head start, but they'd catch him. This wasn't the 1800s. There was technology and modern conveniences these days. Whitmore could get a fixed-wing aircraft airborne in a matter of a couple of hours if he deemed it necessary. He could network with the Texas Highway Patrol, local sheriffs and constables, city police, news media, you name it.

Percy pulled out a pair of reading glasses, bifocals actually, and pondered over the information. He reached in his side desk drawer and opened a box, pulling out a special Cuban cigar. Not easy to come by in this neck of the woods, and not that long since the Cuban missile crisis to boot. Nevertheless, he had his sources, and it was one of the very few vices he permitted himself these days in his pursuit of good health and a clear mind. He mused that various law enforcement officials were out with posses beating the cactus and mesquite bushes, looking around every rock and crevice for this fugitive.

With a slow, calculated change of presence, Whitmore checked his breath. His eyes squinted slightly in revelation, and those squints branched off into the crow's feet wrinkles at the outward corners of his eyes. At last, he let out a cloud of smoke, completely, and set the cigar down in an ashtray. Jim Conklin. Jim Conklin was a local man in that area, and Percy Whitmore had worked with him on occasion. Good man—cool head, good savvy, charisma. No rash moves. Perceptive. Perhaps one of Ranger Whitmore's best resources was laid up in the Van Horn, Texas, hospital. Well, he'd just take a drive over there, maybe stay the night, and do some sniffin' on that trail near the Sierra Diablo and Guadalupe Mountains. An old, familiar tingle ran down his spine. Somehow, he knew this wasn't going to be a run-of-the-mill manhunt. Somehow, he discerned that Trooper Jim Conklin was going to shine a light in areas he didn't as yet know about…

CHAPTER 6

Sierra Diablos—Devil Mountains

Jim Conklin sat up in his hospital bed, looking out the window at the hot day that was near noon. He had heard about Joe Mack on the television set in his room, and he wondered what that young man's chances were of getting out of this mess intact. The scenario wasn't good, and bad news and reputations spread like the plague in West Texas.

He had heard that a Texas Ranger out of El Paso, Percival Pinkerton-Whitmore, was made the ramrod of this endeavor. Conklin had met him a time or two, collaborating on some cases. Whitmore had already solicited the assistance of military troops at Fort Bliss. This consisted of a helicopter, a ground crew, and a squad of searchers to add support to the local posses.

"Mr. Conklin, you have a visitor," Nurse Maria Calderon greeted him cheerily. Heck, Conklin remembered Maria since she was just a kid riding the school bus; now she was a full-grown woman, and a pretty one to boot. She had a slender, shapely figure, and sort of a cute perky looking hairstyle, sort of short, like an airline stewardess might wear. Mostly he knew her and the Calderon family, well enough to know that she had a heart of pure gold and a smile that could break through the hardest of characters.

Maria motioned toward a figure near the doorway with starched and pressed blue jeans, manicured by city professionals, but weathered by the sun and the wind as well. He wore a small badge on his Western-cut sport coat—Texas Ranger.

"Come on in an' have a seat," Conklin invited in a robust tone. "Maria, is there any chance you could find my guest a cup of coffee?"

"I think I can do that," she smiled, "I'll just put that on your bill, Mr. Conklin!"

"Careful now, you don't want to impact the taxpayers in the great state of Texas!"

Whitmore extended a hand of bronzed skin which contrasted sharply with the snow-white linen appearance of the pressed shirt he was wearing under his jacket. He had a strong grip and paused a bit on the handshake to convey confidence, strength, and sincerity.

"Howdy, Jim," Percy greeted him solemnly.

"Howdy, Perc, my goodness, you've got a high-profile assignment this time, don't you? Long time no see—how ya been?"

Whitmore smiled slightly to one side and responded with a twinkle in his eyes, "Well, a might site better than you, apparently! How boogered up is that leg of yours?"

"Ah, heck, not much more than a skin prick—missed the bone and the major arteries. They're just making sure there isn't any infection, once I'm clear in that department I'll be good to go."

"Here you go, Mr. Whitmore," Maria greeted, handing Percy a cup of coffee from the cafeteria. "How about you, Mr. Conklin? Could you use a refill?"

"Wall, darlin', I'd love one, but the problem is that it'd make me have to pee again, and I don't like usin' that dad-gummed portable urinal!"

"Well, I suppose you could just hold it until you're better," she teased, then left the room giving him a wink.

Percy Whitmore was almost expecting her to say "Señor" instead of "Mister," and her Spanish dialect was indeed evident though her command of the English language was quite refined.

"Let's cut to the quick, Jim. What do you know about this Joe Mack fella?"

The smile vanished from Conklin's face, and he returned to a contemplative gaze out the hospital window. Whitmore knew that Conklin wanted to be back in the action, back on the chase in some capacity or another. After all, there wasn't that much fun in handing out speeding tickets on the highways all day long. And the comforts and novelty of lying in a hospital bed wore off quickly for most men. Conklin faced Whitmore with a rather placid expression and replied,

"I don't think that youngster did anything wrong at all."

"Then how's come you're lying here with a bullet hole in your leg?"

"Always two sides to the story, Perc. For all I know, he might've been throwin' a little lead just to get himself some breathing room and hit me by accident."

Now Whitmore gazed out the window for a moment, processing his thoughts before jamming in a quick response.

"The report I read says he was a Marine Corps sniper in Viet Nam—not just any run of the mill Marine I don't think. I know what them ole boys can do—and you think he misjudged his aim?"

"I know that kid, Percy. Hell, we drink coffee together sometimes up at the Pine Springs Café. That boy wandered onto a terrible scene at the worst possible time and probably responded to it in a less than rationale way. That scrappy country bumpkin hasn't been out of West Texas his whole life, save for some summer camp in Southeast Asia."

"War can change a man, Jim—I know. I did time in Korea in the Chosen Reservoir."

"So you were a jarhead, too?" Conklin quipped, amused. "Seems to me then you ought to be more understanding of one of your own! You know, birds of a feather and all that, Semper fi, and esprit de corps!"

Conklin knew the almost cult-like loyalties and camaraderie of those who had served honorably in the Corps; his father had served in World War II when he was just a toddler and had returned with one less leg and shrapnel in his body from the attack on Iwo Jima.

"Sometimes, I don't think I know anything, Jim. I am here to get educated—will you help me?"

"Sure I will, but I got to tell you something."

"What's that?"

"I've worked with you a couple of times, but I *know* Joe Mack. That kid didn't rape that Flores girl and choke her lights out. I've worked this sector for more than ten years now. We're bull raggin' this kid while a rapist-murderer is lettin' the West Texas wind dust over his trail."

"I hear what you're saying, Jim," Percy replied leaning in closer in earnest. By now, he was so close that Conklin recognized his after-shave—Old Spice—the same brand he used. Must be a cop thing...

"He's still got to be caught up to and questioned; there is the matter of that hole in your leg. I'm open to the idea that the real killer may have gotten away. I've got investigators going over the area with a fine-toothed comb. We've dusted for prints at the Flores residence, talked to folks at the Salt Flat Café and the Gas Camp, Dell City School, their friends, people they go to church with..."

"I know," Conklin sighed. "Just do me one favor though?"

"Name it."

"Keep me in the loop. Take whatever you hear from the sheriff's department boys in Hudspeth County with a grain of salt. We don't need a bunch of trigger-happy fools jumping to conclusions or we'll have not only a cold trail, but a dead end."

Percy Whitmore nodded and touched at his jacket where some cigars were stashed in the inside pocket, them remembered he was in a hospital and thought better of it.

"I hear it's suspected he headed into the Guadalupes then?" Whitmore queried.

"Yeah, that's what they think," Conklin countered. "I said he's a good kid, I didn't say he was stupid. He could just be rock hoppin' through the Sierra Diablos while everybody's looking in the wrong place."

"Could be," Whitmore acknowledged, "Then again, could be you just want a bunch of the mob to believe that possibility and back off of that boy's trail a bit."

Conklin didn't reply, but just gave a knowing smile. Both men looked out the window at the southern end of the rugged Sierra Diablo mountains—Devil Mountains in English. Aircraft, jeeps, and searches aside, it could be hell to pay tracking a savvy man in that country. Especially a well-trained, athletic young man with a whole lot to lose by getting caught and a whole lot to gain by distancing his pursuers.

The Apache chief, Victorio, had his last skirmish on U.S. soil in those mountains at Rattlesnake Springs. Victorio and his band were the same as soldiers in these days—they needed water.

Colonel Benjamin H. Grierson, commander of the 10th Cavalry Regiment had beaten Victorio to Rattlesnake Springs. Desperate and tenacious, Victorio and his band attacked Grierson and his black troopers several times before conceding defeat and crossing the Rio Grande back into Mexico.

Crossing the Rio Grande into Mexico. Could be Joe Mack had the same thing in mind. A replay of Victorio's tactics from days of old. Jim Conklin meditated on it a bit. No doubt Joe Mack knew both of the ranges, but likely the Guadalupes a bit more. Still, if one could negotiate the Sierra Diablos to the south, it really wasn't that much farther to Mexico...

CHAPTER 7

A Hard Trail to Follow

Joe Mack had been up while it was still dark and made up a cup of coffee—instant coffee. Quicker and more tactical. He ate a little something cold from his pack, rolled up his bedding, and went down to where Strawberry had been hobbled.

The weight of Joe Mack bearing down on the stirrup made a familiar creaking sound in the saddle leather as he grabbed the saddle horn with his left hand and swung his right leg over Strawberry's back.

He would cross the highway again, get a little south of the Pine Springs Café, and turn Strawberry loose. He knew of an old shed by a water source that the Federal Aviation Administration had put in years ago; there he would stash his tack gear—with a note for whatever friend of his might find it. From there, he would hike back up to the café and make a phone call. He had considered Nickel Creek, which was five miles from Pine Springs toward Carlsbad on Highway 62/180, but the Pine Springs store would likely be busier with highway customers and he could be a bit less conspicuous. It was a bold move, but it was the only way he knew of to make a call. If all went well, he'd catch a bus there, as it stopped by every day, and make a hard trail for law enforcement to follow. They wouldn't suspect anything as outrageous as for him to catch a bus, especially when he could elude them quite handily on horseback or, better yet, afoot, in this vast, rugged backyard of his in West Texas.

Mack changed from his "cowboy gear" into his Marine Corps fatigues, an extra pair of which had been in the pack he'd brought from the trailer. It was a common sight to see servicemen in this part of the country, either affiliated with the Army base in El Paso, coming home from or going to Viet Nam, Germany, or connecting to a flight or a bus to some other base on the mainland. He patted Strawberry on the neck and bid him farewell in gentle, soothing tones.

The old lug-sole jungle boots were still comfortable as he laced them up snug for the walk down the highway. He bloused his trousers with a pair of elastic boot bands to the top edge of his boots. Still had his military bearing and, of course, he had to appear authentic. It would have been more common to be in dress uniform if he was home on "leave," but this would have to do.

Even though he had shaved off his close-cropped beard at the trailer and was wearing a uniform, it was with a high level of anxiety that Joe Mack walked up to the phone booth at the Pine Springs Café. It was just about sunup, and Joe was hoping and praying that Cassie would still be home getting ready for work. There were a couple of pickup trucks in front of the café, which sat just along Highway 62-180 at the top of Guadalupe Pass. There was a military jeep there as well, which wasn't all that common, but seen on occasion these days.

He set down his pack and fished out some change for the phone. This wasn't the time of day he had promised, but there was no time to waste.

"Hello?" she answered

"Cassie, it's me," Joe began.

"Joe, what's going on?"

"Did you hear the news?"

"No, but a friend of mine at work did and told me about it—Joe—"

Joe cut her off quickly, "Cassie, I can't stay on here long, but I can tell you that I came up onto that terrible scene at Flores' by happenchance, and I guess I kind of panicked. I'm on the run for something I didn't do."

"What about the shoot-out at Salt Flat?"

"I don't know what you heard, but I was involved in that."

"Do you realize you shot Jim Conklin in the leg?"

"Conklin? No! Anyway, it was an accident; I didn't mean to shoot anybody."

Four soldiers in green fatigues came out of the café, shuffling about, all of them with a paper coffee cup in hand. A couple of them sat down on a homemade wooden porch swing at the front of the building and were looking at a map or something. The jeep was equipped with a large radio antenna. Suddenly, a scary thought occurred to Joe Mack that these guys might be assisting law enforcement in looking for him.

"Joe, are you still there?"

"Uh, yeah, I was just watching something. Cassie, I've got to get out of here fast, I'll try to call you again soon. You are, uh, alone—aren't you?"

"Yes," she replied with a slight undertone of hurt in her voice that he should ask such a question.

"Good," Joe replied, not for certain whether he believed her or not, but desperately hoping she was telling the truth.

"Let me tell you this much, Cassie—this is important—write it down in case something happens. I can't prove a thing, but I might have an idea who killed Aubrey. I saw a boot heel track by their house, same as one I saw at the Salt Flat Café earlier. There was this Mescin fella in there I thought looked awfully uneasy, apparently paying for gas. He had a sign on his truck, "Quiones Wool Buyers."

"Joe, why didn't you just tell somebody that?"

"Well, I was trying to, but things just got messed up. I never even seen that guy before, and it's only a hunch. I got caught pulling out of their yard by a couple of Mescins that couldn't speak English, but I'm pretty sure they communicated well enough to put high suspicion on me."

About that time, a bus was slowing down on the highway, coming from the east. It only stopped here about three times a day; he'd have to get on it now.

"Cass, I gotta go."

"Joe, where are you going?"

"I can't say right now. You know I'm innocent Cass—and you're still the only girl for me."

There was no response on the other end, only an uncomfortable silence.

"Cass? Did you mean what you wrote in the letter?"

"Yes, Joe, and I still mean it. I'm sorry, and I believe what you just told me. Please call me again—where are you headed?"

"Cass, I got to go now," Joe ended, scrambling to pick up his pack as the driver wouldn't do more than pause if there wasn't a rider waiting by the road.

Mack hooked his field pack over his shoulder and dug out his wallet in front of the driver, a middle-aged man with neatly combed back gray hair, clean shaven, and wearing dark sun glasses. The man wore a white shirt with a tie and black trousers. He obviously took a professional approach to his profession.

"Where you going soldier—Fort Bliss?" the driver asked.

"No, I'm going to visit family, are you headed to Van Horn?" He didn't bother to correct the driver that he was wearing Marine Corps fatigues; the less he knew the better. Let him think he was in the Army.

"Yes sir, we'll pick up the interstate once we get down there. Keep your money, son, if that's all the further you're going. What the company doesn't know won't hurt 'em. I appreciate what you boys are doing over there in Viet Nam."

"Thank you, sir, much obliged."

There weren't that many people on the bus, and normally Joe might've sat up close to the driver to visit a bit—he seemed like a nice guy. But he sure didn't want to visit now, and the less the driver knew the better—he could be questioned later by law enforcement.

The driver pulled the lever closing the boarding door to the bus, and there was a hiss when he released the air brakes and put the big bus into gear. He wouldn't be grabbing very many gears as he was fixing to head down the pass, and many a trucker had lost control descending that mountain in too high a gear. Brakes wouldn't last for long trying to slow it down either.

The bus seemed so high off the ground after Mack had gotten acclimated to riding in a pickup truck. He slouched down in a seat by the window on the driver's side of the vehicle, not particularly close to anyone by design. He tipped the bill of his cover down over his eyes a bit, acting as though he were going to take a nap.

Soon the driver had descended the pass and was signaling to turn down Highway 54 to Van Horn. It would be about an hour's drive down this paved but narrow and winding secondary highway. Mack noticed a sheriff's vehicle coming up from the direction of Van

Horn—he was glad it wasn't pulling the driver over to ask questions. Funny how something could happen in your life, and now you didn't know who to trust, what you should suspect. The sheriff's car turned and headed up toward Pine Springs. Ironically, Mack's suspicion may have been true about a joint search effort.

With much fear and anxiety, Mack sat in the bus seat as it bounced and wound its way over the skinny strip of asphalt that snaked its way between the Sierra Diablo and Delaware Mountain ranges heading south. On one hand, he was successfully getting just a bit closer to the Mexican border; on the other, he had no desire to flee into Mexico. He didn't know anyone there and figured he stood more than a fair chance of landing a fate worse than the one he had here. He peered out the opposite side of the bus windows at the rugged range of the Sierra Diablos. There were a lot of places to hold up in there, provided the posse wasn't close on your trail.

To the east side of the highway, turkey vultures were perched on the fence posts on an endless line of barbed wire. Their wings were spread out with their backs to the rising sun to pick up the sun's warming rays to get them energized to take flight. They were sort of undertaker birds, cleaning up the dead in various forms. They would soar for hours on end, trying to pick up the scent of something dead in the terrain below. So acute was their sense of smell that the gas companies often looked for groups of them hovering in the air when looking for gas leaks in their pipelines. The pilots of the gas company planes knew that the birds confused the gas smell for rotting flesh; there was a similarity. Joe daydreamed for a moment on simpler moments. He had waved in greeting at one of the gas company planes as it flew overhead, and to his amazement the pilot threw something out the window down to him. It was a deck of playing cards with the company logo on it...

What could sometimes seem like a long hour's ride went way too quickly and Mack soon spied the northern outskirts of the little town of Van Horn. He had to act quickly so as not to arouse suspicion by the bus driver and keep on the move. He had very little money and few resources of any kind. He didn't savor the idea of getting further away from his range of comfort, but it was anyone's guess what strategies law enforcement would take to find him.

As the bus slowed down in town, Mack tapped the driver on the shoulder and asked to be let out in a neighborhood close to a church. He thanked the driver and, noticing that there was a car at the little Catholic church, he decided to gamble on the goodwill of someone there. Mack looked around the area and didn't see much activity on an early weekday morning in the community. Not so many people knew him here, and since he wasn't Catholic, it wasn't likely anyone would know him in the church. He went up the steps and removed his hat before going in. Inside a Hispanic priest was stocking some sort of information rack with pamphlets for the parishioners. He was dressed in black slacks and shirt with a white collar piece, but seemed rather relaxed and casual in how he carried himself. He had looked surprised at Mack coming into the church at such an odd time.

"Good morning, my brother," the priest greeted him warmly, appraising his military fatigues.

"Good morning, Padre."

"Is there something I can help you with?" the priest inquired. He was a clean-shaven man, perhaps in his early to mid-thirties, with jet black hair, dark brown skin, and eyes that had a blend of sternness and compassion.

"Well, sir, I'm making my way home, and I'm a little short on money," Joe began, his face reddening slightly, feeling a little guilty at soliciting a handout, something, quite frankly, he had never done.

"I see," the priest replied, seeming to meditate upon the moment and appraising this strange warrior in camouflage fatigues before him. "You aren't AWOL, are you, Marine?"

Mack took that in with a bit of shocked amazement. This man knew his branch of service, knew the acronym for absent without authorized leave, and apparently sensed that Joe was traveling about on the dodge. Of course, draft dodgers and deserters weren't uncommon in these times, though he was neither.

"Oh, no sir," Mack defended, "I'm not AWOL, and I've done some time over there with honor, sir. I've just been hitchhiking to get home for a visit, and I'm embarrassed to say I'm a little low on funds."

Mack was quickly regretting that he had come in here and didn't want the priest to get any more familiar with him.

The priest extended his right hand toward Joe and said, "I'm Father Mike Arias, what's your name?"

After a micro pause, Joe lied out of necessity, "Johnny Delaney, Father."

Mack didn't like lying, but this didn't seem like a good time to tell the truth, although he was speaking to a man of the cloth. On the other hand, he could gamble on this priest and confess what was going on—perhaps he would maintain confidentiality or provide some sort of refuge. Still, Mack was uncomfortable and wishing all the more that he had never had the audacity to come in here pan-handling from a man of God who probably had limited funds and a congregation of modest means.

They shook hands, and Mack kicked himself inside at being the first to attempt ceasing the greeting. The priest had a strong grip that conveyed sincerity and patience. He held his grip and looked into Joe Mack's eyes with a sense of knowing and discernment.

The church was dimly lit, as obviously there was no service. Somehow, it accented the colors in the few small stained glass windows. The dark, solid oak pews were empty for now and the air was comfortably cool with an evaporative cooler running somewhere. There was the unique, sweet smell of incense still lingering from a previous service.

"So, you need some money? How much?"

"Well, I don't know, really. I hate to even ask—just forget it. I don't want to put you out. Thanks for your time. I really should get going."

Father Mike nonchalantly looked at his wristwatch and replied, "It's almost 11 o'clock. How about if I treat you to lunch? There's a nice little neighborhood Mexican restaurant not far from here."

"Gosh, I don't know, Padre; I don't like mooching like this. I'll be fine, really, I should get going."

"Are you in a big hurry? We could walk there in a few minutes. My treat. You do like Mexican food, don't you," and he paused, "Johnny?" as if he knew full well it was not his real name.

Not wanting to look all the more suspicious, and feeling the desire for a hot meal, Joe Mack relented. What was the worst that could happen? He could be caught by the authorities, in which case he could tell his version of the episode and get it over with. Perhaps they were on the trail of the real killer even now. More and more, he was feeling phony in his fatigues, masquerading as an active duty Marine. He longed to get out of them and into his civilian clothes again.

"Oh, sure, I like Mexican food," he affirmed, "I guess if you insist, I'll accept your offer."

"Just call me Mike," the priest went on, attempting to bring down the barriers of his title and position. "Have a seat on one of the pews. I'm going to put on something more casual."

CHAPTER 8

Bad Medicine

Percival Pinkerton Whitmore sat in the shade of chinquapin oak tree on a seldom-used park bench outside the Van Horn Community Hospital. The air was incensed with the aroma of his Cuban cigar. "Bad habit," he thought, "giving Fidel Castro my business buying these damned cigars." Illegal as hell, of course, buying them, but then there were worse offenses one could indulge in. Still, it was better than all the hippies running around the country these days with their whore house vans, smoking dope, dodging the draft, playing sleazy rock and roll music—pure crap as far as Whitmore was concerned—and screwing up the future generation of bastardized children that they recklessly bred into this world with no intention of being responsible in raising them. Rebels without a cause, most of them.

Whitmore gazed off toward the northwest and the Sierra Diablo Mountains. Just out of sight, an hour north, lay the Guadalupes, and parallel to the Sierra Diablos was the Delaware Mountains. Somehow, Whitmore sensed that Joe Mack was somewhere near his range of vision. What place for sure, no one could know. A preliminary search revealed that Joe Mack had doubled back to his trailer and secured his horse, tack gear, and who knows what other kinds of supplies.

What an outdated tactic, Whitmore mused, taking off on a horse in this modern age. Foolish cowboy, who did he think he was—John Wayne? Still, Whitmore admired the audacity of the youngster doubling back to his abode after the shoot-out at Salt Flat. Some kind of sand, some kind of spunk that kid had. If he had the savvy to go along with it, he just might give this crew a run for the money.

Percy took a pull off the Havana, one of the few decadent luxuries he indulged in, and blew the smoke gently upward so as not to obstruct his vision of the mountains, or the city of Van Horn below for that matter. He picked up a steaming paper cup of coffee that he had obtained inside and took a careful sip. Ah, the temperature was just right. It was in some respects a rather placid and pleasant moment—just sitting out there on a pretty morning, in no particular hurry, enjoying a fine cigar and cup of coffee in the fresh, West Texas air.

There was a conservatively small, well-watered and maintained lawn around the hospital, but within a stone's throw were the typical greasewood and mesquite, which no doubt harbored their fair share of striped-whiptail lizards, scorpions, and tarantulas on occasion. Funny thing, Percy mused, people thinking the desert is so void of life, when actually, it is teaming with it. The Good Lord just made the plants and critters here adapted to a hotter, drier environment. Joe Mack was born to this environment. Perhaps Joe Mack was the scorpion in the bush that was not done delivering a few stings to people who pursued him in reckless haste.

Percy pulled out a small pocket journal and reviewed his notes while a respectable length of ash accumulated on the end of the cigar. Joe Mack, Age: 22 Height: 5'11", Weight: 165 pounds. Occupation: ranch hand. Marine Corps veteran; military occupational skill, 0341, 81mm mortar platoon, sniper. Marital status: separated.
"That's right," Percy thought aloud, "I've got to meet with his estranged wife in Roswell."

Whitmore had learned that she worked in a restaurant there as a waitress; he had her address, work hours, phone number. Could be she could shine some light on the fugitive. Could be Joe Mack would try to meet up with her. Not a wise thing to do, but then fugitives weren't always wise. That's when Whitmore would be ready with his tactical snares and network of law enforcement and military contacts.

Whitmore resumed studying his notes, tipped back his Stetson and put the book back in his shirt pocket. There was a peculiar feeling in him about this case—somehow it stirred something inside him. It was easy from his position to almost forget the anguish of the Flores family, and the horrible, irreplaceable loss of a loved one. In some ways it was more senseless, more brutal, without possibility of any bestowed honor or retribution, like someone who lost a son in Viet Nam. Whitmore planned to go to the cemetery at Dell City to the funeral this afternoon, pay his respects to the family, and perhaps establish a time to meet with them soon after the funeral for any possible grain of information that might support his endeavor.

One thing was for sure, if Joe Mack was innocent, then Conklin was correct about the real criminal's trail getting a dusting over fast. And if some innocent, Viet Nam veteran who served his country admirably was being the fall guy, the real killer was just plain bad medicine and would likely strike again, having gotten away with such a crime free and clear. Still, Whitmore didn't want to be passive in his pursuit; no way did he want to be a blemish on the impeccable image of the Texas Rangers. This boy had shot a colleague of his in the leg—a fellow public servant. What he should have done was stand fast and give account of his side of the story; that would have expedited resolving this case. The heck of it was, Conklin, who would be checking out of the hospital this very morning, held no resentment toward his shooter.

Percy glanced at his watch, then toward the door to see if Conklin was hobbling his way out. Not yet. Against his better judgment, he drifted off to the heart of this case. What happened that afternoon—and it *did* happen in the afternoon—to the Flores girl. In his mind he imagined a man coming up to the house and finding her there alone. Did the man know her? Was it Joe Mack, or someone else? Could it be that there was someone more believable to hate and despise and hunt down like a rabid dog? He imagined the poor girl's surprise, her innocence, her brutal, unwarranted attack for the sake of the rapist's short-lived gratification. Is that all the more value a man put on another person's life these days? But then, it had always been this way, Whitmore mused.

He glanced at his watch, and then took another steady pull on his cigar. With squinting eyes, he exhaled in a slow, relaxing fashion, meditating upon the information he had at hand. He would give Trooper Conklin a ride home and visit a bit on the way to the funeral in Dell City. Afterward, he would go to Roswell, hook up with Cassie Mack and the private investigator that he was working with over there, Charlie Knox. Knox was a seedy character of dubious reputation, but a pit bull of a character in chasing down a lead. It was rumored he'd had a semi-successful business up in Albuquerque until he himself had tested the patience or tolerance of local law enforcement in that city. Word was out that it had behooved him to take up his business elsewhere, with a clean slate and a vision to be in more focused compliance with legal investigative procedures. Could be he had more information than he had already given—if Percy could be there in person—and with some cash money to refresh Knox's memory.

Conklin came hobbling out with a bag of personal effects in one hand. It was apparent he was past ready to exit the hospital and, in fact, wasn't so much as looking behind him. Whitmore snorted in amusement, then commented wryly to Conklin, "You remind me of Chester on *Gunsmoke,*" he said, referring to the western deputy portrayed by the actor Dennis Weaver in a popular television series.

"Well, don't get too used to it, I don't plan on keeping this gimpy gait forever, Perc," he replied with just a touch of chagrin in his voice.

CHAPTER 9

Double back

Joe Mack sat down on a wooden pew at the rear of the sanctuary. An evaporative cooler was running outside; he could hear a squeaky bearing on the pulley and the water trickling down the pads that the squirrel cage fan was pulling air through. He looked around in the sanctuary; it was a little dark inside with only the diffused light coming in through some stained glass windows. The windows had beautiful colored images of Jesus and Mary and St. Francis of Assisi. At the front of the sanctuary was an altar and cross with a statue of the crucified Christ upon it. To the side of one pulpit was a statue of St. Michael, the archangel, and on the opposite side was one of the Virgin Mary standing on top of the world, her foot smashing a snake. Joe Mack didn't understand this faith, but he felt safe for the moment, and his gut instincts told him he could trust the priest.

Father Mike re-emerged from his quarters in the back of the church. He was wearing blue jeans and white athletic shoes and a t-shirt with "Houston Oilers" on the front of it. He had sunglasses cocked up on top of his head, ready to be deployed once they went outside.

The sun hurt Joe Mack's eyes as they exited the church into the blazing, glaring, West Texas sun. Van Horn was a typical West Texas town with Spanish daggers and thornless prickly pear cactus-decorated landscapes, plus a number of Chinese elm trees, though not pretty, hearty enough to survive and provide a bit of shade to the modest homes. The houses were nothing elaborate, some Spanish-style architecture, some territorial- or farm-style homes. It was not a big town, and there was nothing there to make it particularly prosperous other than Interstate Highway 10, which had been put through not long ago.

"It's a nice day," Father Mike mused, fishing for some conversation.

"Yeah, it is a pretty one at that," Joe Mack admitted. It would've seemed nicer if he hadn't on the run from the law and his life in general in a mess.

Under different circumstances, it would have been a pleasant walk with this peculiar priest in a little-known, small West Texas town en route to a free lunch. But was there really anything "free" in this world? Joe Mack wondered. They walked into a neighborhood south of the church and came up to what appeared to just be another house, albeit a bit larger and L shaped. It was a white stucco home with a green metal roof, and there was a parking area that would hold perhaps half a dozen vehicles. On the west and south side of the home—or restaurant—were rows of tall Chinese elm trees. They weren't the prettiest trees in the world, but they seemed to survive almost anywhere, and they provided at least a modest amount of shade. There wasn't even a noticeable sign on the property; it was just a given that the locals knew it to be a neighborhood restaurant—"Tina's" it was known as.

Joe Mack and Father Mike walked across the graveled parking area up to the front door and went inside. There was an elderly Hispanic couple dining at a table for two, and a middle-aged Hispanic woman was wiping down a table which apparently had been vacated. There were only four tables in the small establishment, and a window where to-go orders could be placed.

"Buenas dias, Tina! Como esta?" Mike greeted the woman.

"Muy bien, Padre Mike!" she replied, her solemn appearance transforming suddenly into a cheery smile.

In many ways, it was a piece of Old Mexico plopped down in a small West Texas town. Mike ordered an enchilada plate, while Joe Mack got his favorite, chili rellenos.

The kindly padre insisted on paying for the lunch, and they both ordered unsweetened ice tea with a wedge of lemon.

An elderly Hispanic woman came to their table with some chips and salsa, and with some restraint Mack started in on them with a ravenous appetite. Mike muttered something in Spanish to the woman at the counter, then gestured to Joe Mack with a wave of the head to join him outside for a cigarette.

They exited the house and took advantage of a lone bench out on the porch. Father Mike slipped a cigarette in his mouth and offered the pack to Joe Mack. Joe accepted, then produced his Zippo lighter for the ignition ceremonies. Man, it had sure come a long way from Southeast Asia when on one occasion he had used it to burn down a village of bamboo huts...

The priest thanked him facially, without words, then took a harried drag or two from the cancer stick. Joe Mack could read in his face and in his eyes that this man had burdens and a past of his own that he was likely wrestling with.

"Tina doesn't much care to have people smoke indoors," Mike commented.

"Well, it's damn sure a bad and dangerous habit, that's true enough," Joe Mack affirmed.

The shade made life much more tolerable in this neighborhood café, and being off the beaten track appealed to Joe Mack at any time, but particularly in light of the situation he was caught up in at present.

Father Mike took a deep drag off his cigarette and held the smoke in his lungs for a long time before exhaling. Crow's feet showed at the corners of his eyes as he squinted off to the north and the Sierra Diablos, obviously meditating on concerns unknown to Joe Mack. After some time, his mind wandered back into the present and in a tone which hinted at some sort of uncanny discernment, he queried, "So, what are you running from, cowboy?"

"Beg pardon?" Joe Mack countered, rattled to the point of nearly dropping his cigarette.

"Oh, nothin', just a feeling. Then again, maybe I'm just contemplating my own life."

Joe Mack determined that it was time to go; this priest would start to read his mind in pretty short order, a skill he didn't need to deal with right now. He'd have to keep stacking one lie on top of another, and that was a dangerous thing to be doing in his situation.

"Thanks so much for the grub, Padre, but I've got to be shoving off," Joe Mack announced.

"Hey, it was my pleasure, hombre," Mike said, extending his right hand to shake Joe's hand.

Joe sensed sincerity in his grip and, more importantly, in his eyes. He sensed this man was desperate for a friend who could be real, someone to share his burdens with. That was unlikely to happen with Joe, and it certainly wasn't likely to happen now.

"So, where did you say you were headed—El Paso?"

"I don't guess I did say—when's the next bus come through here anyway?" Joe asked, evading the question.

"Next one won't be here until about six o'clock. Why don't you come back to la casa and cool your heels until then? What could you do for the next several hours but be bored otherwise?" he offered.

On one hand, Joe Mack reasoned that to accept his offer would look less suspicious and desperate on his behalf; on the other, maybe this priest would pry and get more information out of him. Maybe he'd even fink on him to the law or something. Going on his first hunch, however, he accepted the offer. One thing he knew for certain, though, was that he wasn't El Paso bound, or Las Cruces, Tucson, or anywhere in between. No, indeed. What he intended to do as soon as possible was to double back. He'd light ashuck of the dumpy little interstate town and drift back into the ranch country to the south of the Guadalupes. Any chance encounter there more likely than not would be with a friend of his. Besides, he knew where the water sources were, good spots to camp, and he could slip into the remote and rugged back country of the Guadalupes when the time was right.

The house, or "la casa," was just sort of an apartment at the back of the church. The meager dwelling consisted of a tiny kitchen that blended into the dining/living room area. It had one bedroom and a bath and a tiny covered porch out the back door.

"Mi casa es su casa!" the jovial priest announced with his arms spread wide, then sweeping one down low with a bow, "My house is your house."

Joe Mack kind of didn't like the fact that this padre's personality was growing on him. Friendships—true ones—were best cultivated slowly and with great caution.

There wasn't much to the living quarters to merit a tour. He noted a crucifix on one wall with a picture of Jesus on one side and Mary on the other. A small desk was along one wall, and just above it were some pictures. One was Mike with a young woman; he had his arm around her—perhaps a lost love? Joe never could comprehend the sense in the Catholics not allowing priests to marry—it defied human nature to Joe. There was also a picture of some young Latino-looking ballplayer in an El Paso Sun Devils uniform. Forgetting his manners, Joe Mack had leaned closer to examine the photo of the pitcher on the mound when Father Mike explained, "That was me before I blew my arm out pitching in the minors. Never got a glimpse of the major leagues."

"Sorry to hear that," Joe Mack replied, somewhat surprised and amused.

"So from there you got some spiritual inclination?"

"No, not exactly. From there I got my draft notice and a couple of tours in Viet Nam."

"But you wanted to play pro baseball—that was your big dream in life?"

"One of them, I guess. I missed the boat on that one, and my high school sweetheart married a buddy of mine while I was off in 'Nam. Dreams are like smoke, cowboy, and they don't remain intact very well in this West Texas wind. Then there was Viet Nam—you know that one—you've been there. I feel sorry for those poor South Vietnamese. It's a horrifying situation with the communist North coming down on them with China's support. Sometimes I wish I could flush that toilet full of memories I have in my mind from those two tours. Of the friends I saw get killed or die slow, the lines of people fleeing to the South away from the Viet Cong."

Mike was getting that distant look again, when he seemed to mentally shift gears with great discipline and asked, "Should we sit outside and have a beer?"

"Sure, that sounds good," Joe Mack responded, his mind racing to piece together the composition of this man who so freely extended his hospitality.

Outside on the patio with a couple of ice-cold Budweisers in their hands, they sat in some rickety wicker furniture. Off to the side was a tiny garden with a few tomato and pepper plants, jalapenos. A cucumber vine crept up a trellis, and there was a little cement statue of St. Francis of Assisi amid the plants. There was a steel bar mounted on one end of the porch which Joe Mack surmised was likely for doing chin-ups.

For a while they sat in silence, just taking in the serenity and momentary respite from the cares of the world. They stared blankly as a checkered whip-tail lizard moved jerkily in and out of the shadows before pursuing successfully a bug that was walking along in the sun-bleached rock and soil on the outside edge of the garden patch.

Joe Mack became mesmerized watching the lizard pursue its prey, oblivious to the two men watching it from the shadows of the patio porch roof.

"Here, have another," Mike offered with a bottle extended. It didn't seem to matter if Joe Mack wanted one or not; the amicable priest handed it off then turned away to sit in his wicker chair again. The sedating quality of the cold beer and the West Texas sun soon had them talking about cowboying and baseball, favorite food, and Viet Nam.

They hadn't meant for it to happen, but they both dozed off in their little outdoor sanctuary. Mike awoke first and pondered a minute before going inside to do something in the tiny kitchen. Soon, he had a fire going in an old metal barrel outside with a metal grid on top. He alternated tending the wood fire and prepping food in the kitchen. He didn't know what this cowboy's story was, but he was going to let him sleep a while.

Joe Mack awoke to the smell of fajitas cooking on the crude grill. He shook off some momentary confusion before gaining his recall.

"You missed the six o'clock bus, cowboy," Mike commented, somewhat amused. You might as well have some chow now; it's a long time until the midnight bus comes, or better still you might as well stay until morning. You can sleep on the couch in the living room if you like."

The food smelled tremendous to Joe Mack as he tried to clear his head. Did they have four or five beers each before he drifted off to sleep? No matter now, his host seemed immensely pleased to have some company of a kindred spirit and past. Had he wanted to call the law he could certainly have done so while Joe Mack slumbered. Perhaps this priest with the tormented past wasn't really all that complicated after all.

Soon he was handed a plate with beef fajitas, strips of beef, onion, and jalapeno peppers. There were flour tortillas, refried beans, and a slice of avocado. The bachelor priest was a pretty good hand in the kitchen; that was obvious, right down the lettuce and tomato salad garnishing one end of the plate.

"Iced tea?" Mike asked. It was apparent to both of them that they had consumed enough beer for one outing.

"Sure, thanks," Joe Mack replied.

"So, what's the plan? Midnight bus, or spend the night and get an early start in the morning?"

Joe Mack contemplated for a bit. It would be of little advantage to travel by bus in the dark and head out into the countryside where he might get snake bit. He would take up the offer and wait until morning.

"You've been too kind," he replied. "There's nothing in this for you—all this generous hospitality. Sure, I'll take you up on your offer, but then I've really got to get going in the morning."

"Hey, brother, I'm just sowing seeds hoping to reap a harvest when the Good Lord calls me home. Besides, I like never get company. And there's like an unseen barrier between me and people in my congregation. They can't seem to separate the man from the cloth."

Later that evening, Joe Mack curled up on the couch with a blanket. He was surprisingly comfortable for the moment, but wished he felt he could trust this priest with the truth of his situation. No, better to keep the man ignorant, especially if law enforcement types should inquire somehow later on. That way, he wouldn't have to lie about anything.

The morning sun greeted Joe Mack peering through the window of the door leading to the patio. Father Mike was preparing coffee and huevos rancheros. One thing was for sure, Joe Mack would leave here well fed.

After breakfast and offering profuse thanks, Joe Mack extended his hand. He might never see this man again, but it had been a special encounter.

"Here you go, cowboy," Mike offered handing Joe Mack a twenty dollar bill.

"No, I couldn't, you've done too much already, and I doubt if I'll ever be this way again."

"Don't worry about it—take it. You'll need it on your journey. And I do pray you get resolution to whatever is haunting you."

Joe Mack accepted the money and noted there was some sort of holy card inside. It was a picture of Jesus on the cross, with some prayer on the back.

As if to explain, Mike said, "He's your ticket hombre—Jesus. Just remember that."

"I'm afraid I'm kind of a back-sliding Baptist," Joe Mack countered, "as I no doubt demonstrated last night out on the patio."

"Ah, a tea-totaling Baptist, eh?" Mike laughed. "As you can see, we Catholics have no qualms in having a drink or two!"

"No, I guess not," Joe Mack concurred. "I've got to make trail, Padre," he said as he extended his hand once again. "Who knows, maybe someday, somehow I can return the favor."

"You already have, my friend. I enjoyed the visit immensely. Stop by again when you get out of this trouble you're in. Vaya con Dios, mi amigo."

And with that, Joe Mack departed, headed north toward the Guadalupes.

Joe Mack didn't look back at Father Mike, but he sensed that the priest watched him until he was out of sight. Joe Mack intentionally switched directions once he figured the priest he had briefly befriended could no longer see him. Ignorance was indeed bliss, after all. Should Mike be questioned later, he couldn't honestly give information on where Joe Mack was headed.

CHAPTER 10

CHARLIE KNOX

Charles, "Charlie" Knox had a gray, weathered sport coat that likely hadn't visited a dry cleaning store in quite some time. He had just lit his seventy-third cigarette of the day and had torn up a respectable portion of a quart of whiskey already. The side effects of his addiction were evidenced in the commode earlier, as he had bleeding hemorrhoids. His eyes were bloodshot and the small veins on his cheeks and nose were inflamed, giving his pock-mocked skin a somewhat sunburned appearance. Percy Whitmore extended his hand in greeting, hoping he wasn't transmitting any facial clue as to the rank aroma that Knox emitted. Obviously, Knox was a man used to scrapping and brawling, grubbing through the dirt and scrub brush like a badger in the desert after a prairie dog. He wore slacks that seemed out of place in the Southwest, more fitting to urban America, but he compensated somewhat with some beat-up black roper-style boots on his large feet.

Knox's office was no prize either, a tiny office upstairs above a struggling department store. It was a tall, skinny staircase climb to his office, and across the hall were a couple of humble apartments, one of them vacant, the other inhabited by Knox. He had a beat up, secondhand oak desk—dusty where you could spy a bare spot— stacked with papers and photographs in no apparent order, a telephone, and a couple of old wooden chairs besides his own, which had likely come from a secondhand store. The heat was oppressive, and it smelled of old papers and books, varnish, cigarette smoke, and sweat.

With restraint, Whitmore refrained from looking at his own hand after exchanging a salutary handshake. Knox's efforts at projecting a somewhat business, professional image ended after the sport coat and battered necktie. Understandably, Knox seemed reluctant to give out copious amounts of information to this Texas stranger, although some financial incentive had been discussed.

"Coffee, Mr. Whitmore?" Knox offered. Whitmore really didn't want any coffee, but instincts told him it would be akin to smoking a peace pipe with an Indian, so he accepted Knox's hospitality.

"Thank you, uh, is it Charles or Charlie?"

"Charlie. Or just Knox—you can call me what you want, just don't call me late for dinner!" he joked flashing a grin with teeth stained by nicotine and coffee over many a weary year.

"Amen to that," Whitmore agreed with a nod and a smile to one side. "And thanks for doing some legwork for me on this Cassie Mack. What can you tell me about her and her ex-husband—Joe?"

"Estranged husband, not ex, not yet anyhow. She's a pretty little filly; I can see where many a man would try to hustle her after she got off work at that café. Tempted myself, but hell, I ain't no spring chicken anymore, and I know I'm not much to look at!" he laughed.

"She had some fling with some oil field trash workin' on a drilling rig. Last I knew he was in jail over in Seminole on drunk and disorderly charges, assaulting an officer, and contempt of court. Lovely individual, just lovely. What the hell does some pretty little heifer with a husband who worships the ground she walks on see in a piece of trash like that, Mr. Whitmore?"

"Sir, I surely don't know. When you figure women out, you give me a call, will you? And you can just call me Percy; I'm sort of uncomfortable with the "mister" title.

"No problem—Percy!" Knox beamed.

"Worships the ground she walks on?" Whitmore queried.

"She said so. Of course, I haven't heard his side of the story—maybe I never will if those West Texas gun hands get too trigger happy. I know I'm not too polished of an individual, Mr. Wh—Percy but one thing I do have is savvy. It don't take a rocket scientist to nose around a little and get some character references. For God's sake, the man's a veteran, and from what I gather a pretty good ranch hand. Nothing unusual to report from his high school days in

Dell City either. Just your run of the mill, West Texas country bumpkin that likely stumbled onto to some sleaze ball's crime scene—not his own."

"You're that confident, are you?"

"That's how I see it—pretty simple, really."

"What do you recommend I do from this point?"

"Talk to Cassie Mack for starters—she's right smart to look at. Workin' right now over at the Yellow Rose Café, but she'll be off in a few hours."

"I'll do that just to satisfy my curiosity—in regard to her husband, that is. I have a wife in El Paso, Charlie."

"Sure," Knox grinned, adding on, "I'd try to cool the trigger fingers somehow on that bunch you've got pounding the trail in the Guadalupes. Some scum bag's out there running around scott free while the West Texas wind's busy dustin' over his trail. That's my opinion. Anybody'd rape and murder an innocent little ole girl ought to be hung by his balls and staked to an ant mound in my opinion. I ain't too polished Mr. Whi—Percy—but that's my opinion, sir."

"I respect your opinion, Charlie. You're not the first to come to that conclusion, but you realize I have to be very thorough in my fact finding. This Cassie—is she staying with some other ole boy now? Any other romantic interest in her life?"

"Not that I've seen. Oh, there's the occasional smooth talker that likes to come into the café, mostly to see her. Naw, I've cased her apartment; she's staying alone these days. Has sort of a sad look in her eyes, too."

"Has she made any plans to meet up with Joe?"

"I asked that very thing, Percy, that very thing. She claims no, but I could tell she was lying. My bet is they're fixin' to rendezvous somewhere, maybe patch up things in their marriage. More power to 'em in my opinion. It's a miserable thing, loneliness, trust me, I know."

"Sometimes it's a challenge being in another person's company as well, wouldn't you agree to that?"

Knox gave him a quick study, jumping to assumptions about Percy Whitmore and his wife, but only silently nodded in agreement.

The two fell silent for a moment, and only the sound of a small portable fan blowing could be heard, and the rattle of the protective wire cage as the fan oscillated. A dusty, taxidermy mule deer trophy adorned the wall behind Knox's desk. Whitmore didn't know whether Knox had bagged it, or if it had come with the place left by a former occupant. He didn't want to ask and get off on some rabbit trail with this investigator with time at such a premium.

Whitmore reached inside his sport coat pocket and pulled out an envelope and handed it to Knox. "Much obliged for your help, Charlie. Here's a little something to keep the bill collectors happy. Keep me posted, and keep track of your time. Maybe we'll just pull off a happy ending to this thing, God willing."

"Maybe," Knox stated accepting the check, "could be God just don't bother himself with every little problem that simple folk get involved with."

"Oh, I do pray you're wrong on that one, Mr. Knox."

And with that, Percival Pinkerton Whitmore exited the office down the dark narrow staircase into the blinding white light of the New Mexico midday sun. He would go pay that "pretty little filly" a visit at the Yellow Rose Café.

Charlie Knox loosened his tie and put his feet up on his desk as he opened the envelope containing the check for services rendered in assistance to the Texas Rangers. The thought of Charlie assisting such a prestigious institution appealed to his ego, and the money would come in awfully handy as well. He'd give this spit-and-polish Texas Ranger a little space, let him visit with that cute little sandy blonde waitress. But in due time, Charlie would be hot on her trail. There would be no other distractions; he'd take on no other cases until he followed her to the inevitable rendezvous with her estranged husband. He laced his fingers in support behind his neck and chewed on a number 2 lead pencil. He meditated a bit; it was something he had the luxury of doing these days. He had just enough time to rustle up some grub for supper, maybe even take a shower—then get back on the trail. Shower. He discerned that Percival Pinkerton Whitmore had some level of aversion to his hygiene, although he was polite and discreet enough. Still, Whitmore's very aura with his liberal application of Old Spice cologne and his starched and pressed creases in his Wrangler jeans and finely manicured mustache and fingernails...well, he just projected an image of a man who attended to the finer details in life. Man like Whitmore could be quite the lady's man—if he wasn't married. Knox smirked to himself.

"Hell, he could be quite the lady's man any darn how!" he mused.

Knox fished a bottle of Old Crow out of his desk drawer and took a generous swig. His eyes glassed over as he fidgeted with his ring finger. There was no ring there now, but there was a scar from where one had once been. He recalled taking a soldering iron to it, nearly burning it into his flesh the day his wife left him without ever turning back...

CHAPTER 11

THE FACE THAT LAUNCHED A THOUSAND SHIPS

Cassie Mack looked distraught, though beautiful, as her troubled eyes looked out the immense span of glass into the glaring Southeast New Mexico sunlight. The supper crowd was already thinning out when a distinguished-looking gentleman in Wrangler jeans with sharp creases and a well-groomed mustache walked in. The hostess seated him in Cassie's section, and he looked at a menu with an air of distraction.

Cassie was distressed over what was going on with Joe Mack—it was a nightmare, really, and in no small manner, her fault. If only she were there—if only she'd never left with that rig hand from Hobbs, New Mexico.

"Good evening, sir, my name is Cassie and I'll be your waitress this evening. Can I get you something to drink while you look at the menu?"

Percy looked up from the menu at some of the prettiest blue eyes, cutest nose, and most voluptuous figure that he had had opportunity to admire in some time. It was not proper that a God-fearing, married man—and professional—such as he should be so enamored.

"Iced tea with a slice of lemon—no sugar please," he replied.

"Iced tea with lemon, no sugar. Got it. I'll be right back," she flashed a smile that was no doubt well rehearsed, but irresistible just the same.

"Actually, I am a might bit hungry," Percy mused to himself. He spied the green enchiladas and figured he'd give them a shot. He felt somewhat sheepish, somewhat juvenile that he had become so immediately infatuated with this perky little lady who should likely best pursue patching up her marriage. He had a job to do, by God, and that was to bring Joe Mack into custody to get some answers preferably alive and well.

Cassie Mack snapped Percy out of his daydreaming as she set down a glass of iced tea with a wedge of lemon nestled on the rim. Percy loathed himself for gazing at the gap in her blouse and admiring the cleavage she unwittingly displayed. For crying out loud, he was nearly old enough to be her daddy; it was an improper distraction at best, even if it could be dismissed as common animal instincts which seem to be the Achilles' heel of many a man.

Percy recalled the tale of Helen of Troy and how she had a face that launched a thousand ships. Surely she had nothing on this fine specimen of a woman, he wagered. He didn't know what brand of perfume she wore, but it was perfect. Not overwhelming, not "5th Avenue," just pretty, just nice.

"Well, have you decided on something, sir?" she queried.

"Huh? Oh, yes, yes, indeed. I'd like to try the green enchilada plate. Does it come with refried beans and salad?"

"Yes, indeed. It has lettuce, tomato, and some avocado."

"Perfect. That will do it. There's only one more thing."

"Yes?"

"I need you to join me in some conversation."

Cassie bristled for a moment, sensing a polished but tacky come on.

"No, no—it's not what you think. I'm Percy Whitmore, Texas Ranger out of the El Paso office. I really need to talk to you about your ex-husband—it's very serious, very official business."

"Oh, I see..." she said softly, looking somewhat deflated. The radiant smile was gone now, and her posture seemed somehow less erect. Yet, from where she stood, there was a bank of windows behind her on the west side of the restaurant, and the sun was glaring in intensely. It radiated in her hair, and although her face was somewhat silhouetted, she appeared almost angelic in appearance.

"Do you need to ask the manager...?" Percy continued.

"Just a minute, er, uh, I think it will be all right. Let me talk to the manager."

She slipped behind the counter and spoke softly to the man who was the manager of the restaurant; they both glanced in his direction. The man asked something, had a pensive expression on his face, and nodded his head quickly in affirmation. Cassie returned to the table and asked Percy for his credentials.

"By all means, ma'am, pardon me. I should've done this to begin with." He produced his badge and a picture ID. Cassie examined them without speaking then resignedly sat down across from him. As she slid into the booth, her knees brushed Percy's.

"Excuse me, I'm sorry..." she offered, blushing a little.

"Oh, no, pardon me, ma'am, no problem at all."

In reality, Percy was glad she had brushed knees; it gave him a vicarious thrill that he didn't seem to want to repel, and that disturbed him, but he couldn't seem to quell it.

Her nose was, well, quite simply, perfect, kind of a little button of a nose, slightly freckled, not too big, and not too small. She had blue eyes and wore her makeup just right. Nothing gaudy, nothing cheap looking, and nothing pretentious either. Absent for the moment was the jolly smile and contagious cheer that he noted when he first came in. That might be hard to resurrect now in light of the situation.

"My husband and I are separated for now, we never divorced," she began. Obviously she detected the erroneous assumption by Percy and wanted to set the record straight. She noted that he wore Old Spice aftershave, the same as her father.

"How bad of trouble is he in?"

Percy knew they were still married; Knox had corrected him on that assumption. So why was he playing stupid?

"Powerful bad trouble, ma'am—the worst. He's suspected of rape and murder, shooting a law officer, resisting arrest, and fleeing from justice. Does any of that shock you?"

"Yes, quite frankly, sir, it does."

"Please, just call me Percy. I'm not some high-ranking officer, but I do pray I at least come across as a gentleman?"

Cassie just looked him back in the eyes. Percy couldn't really read what she might be thinking. When the silence lasted too long, it was he who broke it.

"Has he per chance contacted you about this, er, situation?"

"He called once."

"From where?"

"He wouldn't say. He did claim he was innocent, and that he had a hunch who might have had a connection to the murder/rape of the Flores girl. I believe he said it was Quiones Wool buyers. There was something about a boot heel print that he saw at the Salt Flat Café, then again at the Flores place. I told Mr. Knox all of this."

"Hmmmm," Percy acknowledged, scribbling down some notes on a pad of paper. "Well, Mr. Knox never mentioned anything about another suspect. Maybe he's playing things close to the vest, or maybe he forgot. I don't suppose you'd let me know if he plans on calling you soon, or better yet—meeting up with you?"

"He said he'd call again. Mr. Whitmore..."

"Please, just call me Percy."

"Percy, I don't want him to get hurt. I don't believe he did anything to the Flores girl. After all, we're old friends with that family. I feel so sad for them..." her gaze left his eyes and seemed to fix on nothing in particular outside the restaurant as the sun set in the west.

Percy took another sip of iced tea, noting that he didn't feel rushed as he might have on other queries. Somehow he felt compelled to help this beautiful blonde, blue-eyed girl, no matter the cost.

"What if one of your Rangers or one of the sheriff's deputies gets trigger itch and shoots him, shoots him," she paused a little, struggling, "dead?"

"Miss Cassie, we'll do everything in our power to avoid that. Of course, you can't expect us to dismiss shots fired on us as anything short of a deadly threat to us. Naturally we would return fire. From what I gather, he's no amateur with a weapon—sniper in the Corps, wasn't he?"

"That was different," she jumped in, obviously defensive. "That was war, and that was against communists who had been running rough-shod over people starved for a republic not unlike our own."

"I couldn't agree with you more, ma'am, I served in the Chosen Reservoir during the Korean conflict but he is capable with a weapon, isn't he?"

"Yes, I suppose he is, but he didn't do this crime. It's my understanding someone used their bare hands to commit this crime. With Joe Mack, hands are for work, for love, and for play—like roping competition. Y'all are so busy on his trail that I'm bettin' the real killer has dust covering his trail by now."

"Could be, ma'am, could well be. We'll pursue this lead about Quiones Wool buyers."

"Percy?"

"Yes?"

"Please call me Cassie, I'm not old enough, at least I'd like to think I'm not—to be referred to as ma'am."

"Certainly, Miss Cassie, certainly," he replied in an apologetic tone with sympathetic eyes as he patted her gently on the side of her shoulder. His mind wandered a little longer than was healthy at her attractiveness.

"Are you finished?" she asked.

"Pardon me?"

"With your plate, I mean, are you finished? Would you like some dessert?"

"Oh no, ma—er, uh, Miss Cassie, no dessert, thanks. Everything was just fine."

With that, she rose and took his plate, signaling that the interview was over. Percy noted her slender little hands as she stacked his dining utensils with an efficiency that betrayed her lengthy experience at such tasks. There was no ring on her finger, but then, it might be impractical with her work. In his heart he felt it a shame that she had to work at such a task day after day to pay the bills. She was so beautiful, so nice..."

"In case you learn anything else that could help me bring this to a peaceable resolution, here is my card and my number." He placed it on table with an insanely generous tip, put his hat on, then gave it a little tip in respect toward her as he exited the restaurant.

Cassie Mack left the card and the tip on the table until he had exited the restaurant. She noted the generous amount and that he seemed an exceptional gentleman of sorts. There was something solid and decent in the man's demeanor. That he was a gentleman she had no doubt. That he was kind and courteous in handling the situation she had no doubt. What his agenda was, or what all he was willing to do to achieve it, she could only speculate.

CHAPTER 12

Into Victorio's Stronghold

Joe Mack had hitched a ride out of Van Horn headed north toward the Guadalupes. They were in fact some Mexican farm workers headed back to Dell City, but fortunately they didn't know him. He had them drop him off near a ranch corral, and for all they knew he was a hand there. In reality, Joe was going to "borrow" a mount and hopefully some tack gear to get him nearer to the land he knew so well and could hide in. He had hunted mule deer, coyotes, and mountain lions in this country and had learned a lot of intricacies about the habitat along this skinny ribbon of asphalt called Highway 54.

Some turkey vultures were perched atop the barbed-wire fence posts with their wings stretched out, collecting some passive solar gain with their backs to the sun rising in the east. Like bizarre winged undertakers, they were gearing up to soar the skies in search of something that had died. The gas companies sometimes found gas leaks in this remote region of the country by watching for a gathering of turkey vultures. The chemical that was put in gas had a smell not unlike rotting flesh; at least it seems such was the case with the turkey vultures.

The horse was a black gelding with white stockings and some white on its face. Joe recognized the horse; his name was Chicory, like the Southern substitute for coffee. He would ride Chicory until the next ranch boundary, then abscond with another mount. He rode up by Rattlesnake Springs, watered his mount, then headed east to cross the highway away from the Sierra Diablos and go over into the

Delawares. He kept only the bridle just in case he wasn't so lucky to find a tack room unlocked at the next ranch. He could ride bareback, though he didn't much care for it. The next horse was a sorrel mare named Cupcake, and hers was a gentle spirit he wished he had for his own. He mused how once upon a time he could have been caught by less friendly ranchers and hanged for being a horse thief, never mind the other charges he had against him. Eventually, he came up to the area where he had turned Strawberry loose, managed to find him among a small herd of horses, and swapped out the tack gear. He nudged Strawberry with one stirrup, ever so gently, as he encouraged him up an escarpment in the Delaware Mountains as the majestic Guadalupes loomed ahead in the light of the moon. He paused at the top and dismounted, patting Strawberry on the neck gently, and speaking to him in soothing tones, assuming the horse understood his every word.

"This is where we part trails, ole pard."

Joe wished he could take his trusty mount up into the Guadalupes, make better time. But he knew better; it would cut his tactical advantage nearly in half being on horseback, especially if an air patrol should fly over him. No, he had to do this afoot if he was to successfully elude his pursuers.

He patted Strawberry on the rump and voiced a somewhat stifled "haw" to send the horse more south into the Delawares. He stole across Highway 62-180 with his pack on his back and the palms of his hands sweating.

Cassie. How he would love to hear her voice just one more time. That it was late, there was no doubt, still, he should try. She would be worried about him, of course. It was not that far out of his way to hike over to the phone booth at the Pine Springs Café. There was no better tactical time, as he could approach under the cloak of darkness.

He felt around in his pocket to be sure he had some change. He did. With renewed enthusiasm, he hiked toward the café. Although it was close if one were in a vehicle, it seemed like forever to get there on foot.

When at last it came into view, he stopped to catch his breath and scope out the establishment. The owners were apparently asleep in their portion of the complex. There were buildings adjacent that had at one time been apartments, and even a dance hall. Joe Mack stole up on the phone booth and wasted no time in depositing his change and dialing the number. It rang. It rang some more, and more. Maybe she was asleep, maybe she was out on the town with some other guy, maybe...

"Hello?" came a soft, drowsy query from his beautiful blonde, estranged wife.

"Cassie?"

"Joe, is that you?"

"Yes, now listen, baby, I miss you so much, but I can't stay on the line long. I think they can track these things."

"Who? Who can track things?"

"The police, the Rangers, the FBI I don't know. Listen, I'm all right for now, and I don't want any more run-ins with the law. Have you been able to tell someone about my suspect—about the wool buyer, the boot prints, and all that?"

"Yes, Joe. There's this investigator, Charlie Knox, and a Texas Ranger by the name of Percy Whitmore. I told both of them."

"Texas Ranger? Oh, God, this is serious. But that's good, that's good that you told them. Do you think they believed you—believed me?"

"I'm not sure, Joe—I hope so. It's hard to tell with these types."

"Cass, you got to get them on that trail—on the real killer's trail. I've got to keep on the run until they've made some progress elsewhere."

"Joe, where are you?"

Joe Mack paused a moment then lied, "I'm somewhere near Las Cruces up near the Organ Mountains. But you must not tell anyone, no matter what."

"I won't Joe, I promise. Joe, when can I meet you? Where can I meet you?"

"Not now, Cass, not now. It's too dangerous. I'll get in touch soon. I love you, Cass."

"I love you, too, cowboy."

Then, somewhat abruptly, somewhat quietly, he hung up the phone.

"Damn it!" an agent exclaimed pulling the headset off his ears, "I couldn't quite pinpoint it. It could've been most anywhere in the vast Southwest."

"It's not all a waste," Pervical Pinkerton Whitmore replied, "at least we have a little more intel. We need to get a unit over around Las Cruces and the Organ Mountains and scour that area!"

Joe Mack scoped out the highway from both directions, then hustled across the pavement up toward the Guadalupes. Victorio's Stronghold. It had worked for the wily Apache chief then, and it would work for Joe Mack now. Now and again, he sprinkled some hot pepper powder he had absconded from the unwitting priest in Van Horn. Should they pursue him with dogs from this point, that would put them out of commission for a while.

His pack seemed so heavy. No doubt he was out of shape in contrast to his physique in Viet Nam. Much of the weight was extra water; he would need it until he reached the top. Then, he could likely replenish his water at the tank in The Bowl. The Bowl was so named due to the shape of its terrain up on top of the mountains, and a manmade tank had been dug out and a pipeline placed to pump water from Pine Springs all the way up Bear Canyon and into The Bowl. It was quite the project with the line of steel pipe winding its way up over two thousand feet in elevation gain. Water, after all, was more precious than silver or even gold in this part of West Texas. The availability of water changed a lot of things when it came to survival of either man or beast.

Joe Mack huffed and puffed as the Pine Springs trail grew steeper up the ancient limestone mountains. The Guadalupes, geologists claimed, were the largest exposed fossil reef in the world. It was perhaps the most unique area of geology in the entire Permian Basin. No small wonder it was being added to the National Park System, and already geologists flocked to the area with pick hammers and European hiking boots, shorts and floppy hats.

The moon had crossed over quite a bit of the sky by now; the hour must be getting quite late. It mattered not the time, Joe Mack just chugged some more water, managed to slow his breathing and heart rate, and plodded on through the moonlight. He must reach the dense timber of The Bowl before daybreak, then find somewhere to hold up during the peak daylight hours. Even with the cool night air, he was drenched with sweat from the arduous hike, and the sound of his boots crunching on rock and his gasping breaths seemed to dominate the world of sound on this unusually calm, quiet evening.

With no immediate threat hot on his heels, Joe Mack tended to daydream. He meditated on the days of Victorio and his skirmishes with the Buffalo Soldiers out of Fort Davis in this harsh land known as West Texas. Had the Apache, too, eluded capture and annihilation by traveling through the dark of night into the rugged back country of the Guadalupes? More likely than not, they had, Joe decided. At any rate, he—Joe Mack—was winding his way into one of the last strongholds of the Mescalero Apache—into Vioctorio's Stronghold.

When he thought he could go no more, he decided that he had eased unceremoniously into the high country timber, as he was no longer making a steady ascent. He wasn't certain, but imagined that it was getting somewhat light in the east and that there might be just the faintest of reddish glows along the horizon as he looked off in the general direction of Pecos, Texas. Nearly exhausted from his hasty ascent, he decided to go only a little farther, then stop for a break, eat a bite, and find a good concealed area to catch a wink or two. Breathless, he noted casually a thorny looking Texas horned lizard moving with jerking motions, capturing ants with its tongue. The lizard had its food, Joe Mack earnestly desired just a cup of coffee.

There would be no fire, no hot coffee—couldn't risk the chance of being seen. He had lost a buddy in Viet Nam who had lit a cigarette in the night, only for a Viet Cong sniper to hone in on the tiny glow of the cigarette as he inhaled. A shot to the brainpan made for the way for the mistake to happen only once, the only benefit being to the survivors who had witnessed it.

One could never rule out the possibility of coming across a rattlesnake in this country. Some snake handler that had stopped in at the Pine Springs Café claimed there were actually five different species of rattlesnakes in the Guadalupes. There were Western diamondbacks, black-tails, rock rattlers, Mojaves, and prairie rattlers on the west side. All Joe Mack knew was that if you heard the buzz of a rattle, it might already be too late this far from a medical facility. If it were a Mojave, he would possibly have no more than an hour or two to make his peace with the Lord before he checked out of this mortal world.

With caution he selected a secluded spot to bed down for a bit after a bite of cold rations. Fatigue was overwhelming him. He reflected briefly on how soundly he had slept at the priest's home in Van Horn. There would not be so peaceful or lengthy a slumber here. He was both predator and prey. He must become as wily as a mountain lion, as elusive as Victorio. As he curled up in his bedroll, he could hear a red-tailed hawk screech up in the vast West Texas sky just before the sun would turn the page on a new day. Joe Mack didn't relish sleep out on the ground in this country; too many critters to consider: rattlesnakes, scorpions, centipedes, and black widow spiders. It would do no good to fret about them now, he was too tired, he was...too....

The shriek of a golden eagle overhead startled Joe Mack into semi-consciousness. He quickly surmised that he had been sleeping hard in his little off-trail nest in Victorio's Stronghold. Judging by the sun, it had to be mid-afternoon. In tactical fashion, he kept very still, moving ever so slowly even to look around. On one hand, it was unnerving that he had slept so long in broad daylight; on the other, it was indeed good that he remain out of site, with minimal movement during the daylight hours.

Joe Mack snapped off a stem of side oats gamma grass and chewed on it meditatively. He could see no trace of another living soul anywhere in sight, and he could see for miles in many directions from this vantage point. He looked down on the ground and spotted a dung beetle rolling a ball of cow manure taller than itself. It appeared comically clumsy rolling the despicable round prize through the dusty soil en route to its secret storage somewhere for 'dining' later on. Amazing, the diversity of things that dwelled in the desert.

Johnny O'Grady pulled his pickup truck over along the dusty ranch road and pulled out a pack of smokes that had been tucked in his rolled-up shirt sleeve. A horse had caught his attention, and he was looking in the direction of an earthen tank now where the roan horse was sipping water somewhat nervously. Suddenly, it hit him—he knew that horse—that was Strawberry—Joe Mack's horse. Johnny O'Grady was an old friend of Joe's; they had played cowboys and Indians when they were just kids. They had gone to school together, worked cattle, sheep, and goats together. He was a pretty good artist at pencil sketching and painting and had, in fact, a hankering to pursue such frivolity more fervently, if only there were more money in it. He had heard all the recent news and his thoughts began to race around wildly in his mind. He took a quick look in all directions to see if Joe Mack might actually be here in the vicinity, within eyesight of his horse. Nothing. It was an unusually calm moment, nearly as quiet as a cave. No sign of anyone, not even any cattle particularly close by. Johnny took a drag off his cigarette and exhaled the smoke as he gazed up into the grand spectacle of the Guadalupes. He squinted his eyes in the brilliant desert daylight and exhaled a ring of smoke that encircled Hunter Peak in his eyesight. To his notion—in his own gut—he *knew* where Joe Mack was. He knew as certainly as if there had been an affirming smoke signal from the peak or a neon sign flashing on the next hilltop. The question was what he would tell a law enforcement person should he be asked for his knowledge or even opinion. By all rights, he should report the fact that Joe Mack's horse, Strawberry, was here. He rubbed his bristled chin as his beady brown eyes danced around in intense thought. Without delay, he turned the key in the truck's ignition and slowly drove on.

"What horse?" he asked himself aloud, as if responding to an unseen interrogator.

"No, sir, I haven't seen hide nor hair of Joe Mack in several weeks, nor his horse for that matter."

"How did Strawberry get out here on the 6-Bar? Sir, I haven't a clue. Found a wire down in the fence and wandered, maybe. No, sir, I haven't any idea where Joe Mack could be, most likely El Paso or San Antonio hiding out amid the masses if he's smart. No, he wouldn't stay around here, no sir."

No one had seen it, but had they been looking up in the mountains where Johnny O'Grady had been looking—and looking carefully—they might've seen a glint of light reflect off of a shiny object that a fugitive from justice was brandishing. That object was a high-powered rifle.

CHAPTER 13

THE DEMONS WITHIN

Salvador Quiones had avoided wool buying in the area of Hudspeth County where he had raped and murdered little Aubrey Flores. It was with tactical fear, not remorse or dread, that he dodged the area. He had made up many excuses to his brother and brother-in-law as to why he preferred not to go to that area of late. He claimed there were better, more viable markets elsewhere in the region, and money was the language they spoke perhaps even better than Spanish.

Aubrey was not his first victim; there had been several in Juarez over the years, and the young hitchhiker near Dona Ana, New Mexico, two years ago. She was a pretty little blonde-haired hippie, free spirit, happy go lucky. She wasn't very lucky the day she thumbed a ride toward Tucson and he picked her up. He had raped her out on a desert back road and buried her in a thicket of prickly pear cactus so dense that no one was ever likely to go nosing around. He still remembered her tight-fitting faded bell bottom jeans, tie-dye shirt, and no bra—and that headband. She was from Kansas, originally, as he recalled. It's not that he didn't make small talk before he ravaged and murdered her. After all, she had sort of asked for it—hitchhiking alone, bra-less, flirtatious, and friendly.

Salvador was not a particularly handsome man. He had heavy facial scarring from a bad acne condition when he was a child. He was trim and fit enough, and he had a healthy head of black hair, the top of which was typically covered with a white straw cowboy hat.

He could have a deceptively pleasant smile and jolly demeanor when it suited his needs. A certain amount of charisma, after all, was needed when doing business with clients and potential clients. He could milk a buck out of his gringo clients as well as the Mexicans and Native Americans. Oh yes, rest assured, Salvador Quinoes could be a smooth talker, a real "slick" when he needed to be.

Funny thing about that, though. The last girl, the one the news reporter called Aubrey Flores, she had looked apprehensive when she opened the door and saw him. It had been clear to Salvador that she was expecting almost anyone else but him. He had not done business with the Flores family before, but had been told they had a flock of sheep and a few Angora goats, so he had looked them up. The situation with Aubrey had been spontaneous, like a couple of his episodes in the past. The spoiled little brat. He could tell she had been doted on by her parents, that she hadn't a care in the world. You could feel it in the Flores household—too clean and neat, wholesome and safe. Well, it didn't end up being too safe that day as he dragged her into the bedroom for an education she would never be able to use or share. It was really her parents' fault to some extent; they shouldn't have left a tempting little dish like her alone. They shouldn't have pampered and loved on her and protected her all her life to make her so vulnerable and naive. Shame on her discernment, to so rapidly see the evil in his soul and exhibit her fear. Perhaps if she had come on to him like a thoroughly sleazy whore he would have just had his way with her then let her live. Then again, not likely. After all, he realized, as likely did God himself, that he was a rattlesnake in human clothing.

Pampered, coddled, loved. Safe and secure. Well fed and clothed. It was disgusting, and it was not what Salvador had been accustomed to in his youth. He thought back to those days growing up outside a little village well south of Juarez. He wished he had a fancy U.S. silver dollar for every time his father had molested one of his sisters or knocked his mother around in a drunken stupor. He wished he even had a worthless Mexican peso for all the times his father had berated him and his siblings verbally, or backhanded him and beat on him until he was too tired to continue. The only charitable thing the old devil had ever done was get him drunk on his fifteenth birthday and set him up with a skanky Juarez prostitute. And yet, that wasn't a fond memory either; it was somehow dark, somehow dirty and ugly, somehow degrading. His father had been there watching and drinking and laughing...

Salvador pulled off the highway outside of Anthony, just west of El Paso, took off his hat, and aggressively rubbed his face with both hands. He was starting to sweat profusely and his head hurt. For a fleeting moment he imagined—at least he assumed he imagined—that he saw some sort of human-lizard-like winged demons perched along the rock cutoff to the side of the highway. He knew the demons would have him some day, there seemed no stopping it. He contemplated a bottle of tequila that was in the glove box, then thought better of it. He did not like his life, but he did not know how to change it. He had done many bad things he supposed he could be imprisoned for should the law ever catch up with him. He could move away to another state, but he lacked confidence that he could acquire gainful employment on his own. He had no contacts like he did here in El Paso and Juarez. Here he had freedom and, to some extent, anonymity when his desires raged out of control. The desert was a big place. The cities were a big place. To some extent, you could blend in and vanish in a crowd.

His mother had in vain lit many a candle in the tiny Catholic church in their old village, praying that Salvador and his father would be loosed of the demons that possessed their very souls and being. He suspected she had even told the priest, but that had been in confidence and was likely never mentioned to any law authority.

His vision began to clear as he looked over the dashboard of his pickup truck and spied a roadrunner with a striped whip-tail lizard in its mouth. It would fairly easily swallow that entire lizard for a meal and move on about its business. He studied the bird for some time, noting as he always had that they preferred to run more than fly. The bird had no qualms about killing and devouring lizards, it was a matter of survival. It was no sin for them to kill horned lizards and whiptails. Perhaps it was no sin for Salvador to do what he had done. Perhaps his mother had purchased enough prayers that he wouldn't spend but just a short time in purgatory. But she was no longer alive to make such prayers. Neither was his father alive to torment him or his siblings. Salvador and his brother had taken care of that situation several years ago.

He must be wise and brazen. He must not let on that he was guilty of anything. After all, who could say he was guilty? And according to whom? How he chose to live his life or end others' was his business. If people were stupid, it was their fault that they should die, not his. He would resume his buying trips in Hudspeth and Culberson counties as if nothing had happened. He would feign shock and dismay when customers casually shared the tragic news with him. He would take off his hat and hold it near his chest, then do a sign of the cross with his right hand and pretend he was muttering a little prayer. If need be, for effect, he could even produce some genuine tears from his eyes. That would fool them. That would fool them all. Nothing was any different this time than all the others, and nothing would be any different the next time, or the next...

CHAPTER 14

CASSIE'S MIRROR

Cassie Mack looked in the bathroom mirror and applied her lipstick and mascara. She masterfully applied just the right amount of everything to enhance her natural, innocent beauty. She had to. All women had to. It was the way it was. Women had to be pretty; it was their only safety net, their only defense. It was quite often, at least to the more shallow men, the only way to be good enough.

Reflecting back, she realized with a dull pain in her heart and stomach that Joe Mack was not a shallow man. Be that as it may, that foolish cowboy, he could find her attractive first thing in the morning without any makeup, or worse yet when she had been sick with the flu and ashen, pale. No, then he only saw all the more reason to pamper her and coddle her and build up her self-esteem. He would pamper her like his baby girl and nurse her back to health. He had no qualms about fixing her chicken noodle soup or getting her a glass of 7-Up to settle her stomach. He had cleaned up her vomit without complaint and changed the bedding and laundered it without grumbling when she had been sick. She wasn't sick often, but it had been a profound learning experience every time she had been. When the chips were down, she knew the one person she could count on. An unscrupulous woman would have played sick once in a while just to be doted on so.

In some ways, she just figured he was full of cowboy bullshit and charm, that he was a schmoozer of sorts. He had likely flattered many a girl in his time. Stub Rogers and Johnny O'Grady claimed he could schmooze the devil himself out of steak dinner and a cold beer. And yet, imperfect though he was, he had been loyal to her, and he had tried to understand her, even when he could not possibly do it.

Perhaps it was unfortunate that she had never divulged the date rape she had experienced shortly after their family moved to the booming oil town of Monahans, Texas. She had been foolish enough to believe that one of the football jocks had really seen something special in her when he had asked her out for a date. She had been on top of the world when he had pulled up in the fancy new pickup truck that his parents had bought for him, wearing his brand new jeans, shirt, and fancy cologne. He was immensely handsome, and he had charisma. He had a radiant smile with perfect teeth and wonderful dark brown hair that framed his sparkling blue eyes. Naturally, a piece of white trash like her had been infatuated with him.

White trash. She had referred to herself with that term a time or two in Joe Mack's presence only to be reprimanded for using such a description. She was his princess, and he would listen to no self-degrading talk without chastising her for it. She was wonderful and kind, encouraging, loving and giving, hardworking and beautiful.

Despite his exhorting, flattering nature, sometimes Joe could brood. He had his own demons that tormented his mind and darkened his spirit. When he wrestled them, she questioned his love for her. When she wrestled them, she could see his love for her even through his own hurt, frustration, and confusion. She could have done far worse in life—and perhaps would, if she couldn't patch things up with him. She couldn't lie to herself; certainly she occasionally fantasized about someone better looking, or richer, or with a prominent status in life. And yet, who was she to fantasize such things? Then again, that he occasionally entertained similar thoughts was likely; he was, after all, just a man. And yet, she anchored herself on the belief that ultimately he would forgive her and be committed to her to her dying day. Perhaps they would have children, and someday grandchildren, and this life of current nightmares would become but a blurry, distant memory. Joe Mack would be a wonderful daddy.

She knew things had started with the rape, though Danny Grey was never charged with any such thing. It would have been too humiliating and for all she knew difficult to prove. When her parents inquired why she wasn't seeing him anymore, she made up excuses about him being a spoiled oil field brat whose parents weren't yet used to being rich. While those allegations were true, they masked a more heinous truth. Fortunately, she hadn't gotten pregnant—she had worried about that for a month. Once she overheard heard him bragging about the event by his wall locker at school with his buddies, and they had all had a good laugh about it. It had made her sick to her stomach, and she never could hold her head up in that school again.

No, Joe didn't know about that chapter in her life, or about numerous others that followed in her Godless youth. It was the sixties, God was out and sex, drugs, free love, and rock and roll were in; at least that's what the hippie culture claimed. She wished she could whitewash her past, but that is never possible. She wished she had never slept with another, though she knew that Joe had felt the same about his past.

Occasionally, he would awaken shouting and thrashing about in bed. He was in combat or something too bizarre to divulge. She would always cautiously speak to him, then carefully touch his shoulder with reassurance. It was unsettling to see him troubled, or crying; after all, he was her Superman, he was her savior protector shouldn't he be invincible? Shouldn't he be without flaw?

Then there was this Texas Ranger—Percy Whitmore. Strikingly handsome, professional, somewhat refined. Had she imagined that he studied her with more than casual interest, that he was distracted beyond the case at hand? He was a gentleman. He was much older, of course...Damn! Why did she even entertain these thoughts? The cycle had to be broken, she had to change her ways before the rest of her life was in ruins. And yet, the best candidate on this earth to help her achieve that goal was out on the run somewhere—perhaps in the Organ Mountains near Las Cruces, New Mexico.

She relaxed her hold on the hair brush and gazed into the mirror, mesmerized by memories. Back when the rig hand was making his daily passes at her in the Salt Flat Café, when she was starting to buy the bullshit and welcome the attention. When she had allowed some things more physical than a decent woman should have. Joe Mack had a dream. It unnerved her when he shared it. He named the dream and claimed it felt too real not to have some sense of foreboding. He named it "the tattletale mirror." In his dream, he was at a café counter sipping a cup of coffee when a little Hispanic man looking pensive and without speaking a word showed him a mirror. Joe Mack had looked into that mirror and seen his wife Cassie, standing up on her toes to better reach the rig hand she was kissing. He had awakened in a cold sweat, and the images were branded in his mind just as surely as a young steer had been branded with a white-hot iron.

Her answer was silence when he shared the dream with her, but the look of shock on her face was evident. Joe Mack was not a particularly religious man, but he claimed that kind of dream could come from only one of two sources—God or the devil. He preferred to think it was God's spirit warning him to climb out of his self-denial about the turmoil his marriage was in, to get in the saddle and fight for his fair maiden with emotion and passion and wisdom, and most of all with faith.

Nevertheless, she had left Salt Flat and moved first to Hobbs where she shacked up with the rig hand for a while. It didn't last for too long and, after, she moved to Roswell. Joe Mack had never had the heart or the stomach to ask very many details. Cassie was equally thankful that he didn't ask, for there was no undoing anything she had done.

Could the mirror steal her very thoughts? Could it divulge the darkened smudges on her soul to the next user who casually glanced in the glass? Ridiculous, of course, but then so was life—ridiculous and painful. And complicated. Nothing could be simple, or restful, it seemed. The mirror was only glass, after all, with silver paint on the backside.

She had no immediate family support. Her parents had long ago moved to Bartlesville, Oklahoma, for employment and had dug in there. They had found Jesus, or so they claimed, and encouraged

Cassie to do the same. Testimonies of that sort were not unusual in the Bible Belt; still she wondered if they were true. Of late she prayed for some sort of sign to let her know that God was indeed real. That He even cared at all...

That there were supernatural forces at work in this world she did not doubt. There seemed to be too many things that one could not explain, not the least of which was the alleged UFO crash that had occurred near Roswell years ago. There was the dream that her estranged husband had shared with her. There were times when the infernal wind would blow for days on end in the late winter and early spring that she would look into the mirror getting ready for work and almost hear things audibly. Sometimes the voices suggested that she would be better off dead, that she would never have any kind of a life. Sometimes, she believed, it was suggested that she do it herself, other times the voice seemed to say, "I'll have you!" Was she going insane? Was there any hope?

In the mortal sense, it came in three figures: Percy Whitmore and Charlie Knox on the trail of the truth, and somewhere in the Guadalupe Mountains overlooking the salt flats—Joe Mack, a man with a renewed love and passion for his estranged bride. But Joe Mack was on the run, and the resources mounting against him were formidable. One wrong move, one misinterpreted signal, and he would be dead before any kind of truth could come out.

Cassie stared into the mirror and thought she saw Joe Mack, afoot, somewhere in the Guadalupes with his lever action rifle in his hand. Alone, bucking the sun and the wind and the elements. There was no one else around. There was a pensive look on his face. He appeared determined, yet fearful. In her heart she knew he was determined, yet vulnerable. Gradually, but increasingly louder was the drone of a single engine airplane, a law enforcement aircraft. She was startled by the clatter of her hair brush bouncing on the vanity countertop as she saw a look of horror come across her face, and a feeling of dread engulfed her very being...

CHAPTER 15

LIKE A WISP OF SMOKE

At first Joe Mack thought the airplane was some ranch hands coyote hunting or perhaps park service staff scoping out the new property recently added to their system. Clearer thought soon prevailed and he rightfully assumed that some form of law enforcement was flying around looking for him. They would assume a cowboy would be with his horse; how easy to spot. It was never a safe bet to assume, Joe Mack pondered.

He kept low in some mountain mahogany brush, tactically blending in with the terrain. This skill was better learned in the Marine Corps than what he had come up with playing cowboys and Indians back in the day with Johnny O'Grady.

The drone of the little Cessna prop plane intensified then faded off as it flew over him then continued on in its somewhat random search. Joe Mack's heart was racing, his throat was dry, and an inner sense of panic was trying to overtake him. Right now, panic was his most formidable foe. No one really knew for sure where he was. They were speculating and had little hard evidence regarding his whereabouts.

Slowly turning his head with minimal motion, Joe Mack spied more by accident than anything else a mountain lion padding its way softly along a cliff. The big cat looked in his direction, almost as if it had a sixth sense that told it a human had spotted it. The cat was totally motionless for a while. From the distance, Joe Mack wondered if his eyes were really seeing right. Actually, he had never seen a mountain lion before. He'd heard many stories about the notorious killers of sheep and goats, though the National Park Service employees, (Parkies—he called them), claimed they preferred deer meat. Had his situation been different, he would have been jubilant at the sighting; it was something to be excited about.

With the most subtle hint of movement, the big cat evaporated into the desert heat to be seen no more, like a wisp of smoke carried away in the desert wind. Joe knew that he, too, must be much like the big cat. He must be stealthy and cunning and tough. Should the occasion arise, he must be able to disappear like a wisp of smoke.

The almost lonely sound of the airplane fading in the distance put his mind more at ease. At least they hadn't spotted him. It was time to cover some ground, not good to stay in the same place too long. Moving cross-country was fraught with perils: cliffs that suddenly appeared when you were going down slope, trip hazards, loose rock, and the incessantly abundant agave, or "century plants." These succulent desert plants that the Mescalero Apache roasted just before they shot up stalks were tipped with needle sharp points that were tough as spear heads. Any cowboy, wetback, or hiker in this part of the country had heard accounts of horses or people getting killed who had had the misfortune to fall and become impaled on one of these nasty plants. They were a symmetrical thing of beauty, but one had to watch every footstep lest one of the sharp points poke through your boots and crippled your foot. Something as simple as a crippled foot would end his quest for freedom.

Stealthily he moved through the groves of ponderosa pine and, at the southern extreme, large Douglas fir trees. There was the sweet, somewhat pungent aroma of pine pitch in the hot dry air as he plodded through the mountains, not sure where he was going, only intending to elude his pursuers and keep them in the dark as to his whereabouts. Ah, the high timber above the Chihuahuan Desert below. He heard a rustle of leaves and noticed some wild turkeys walking briskly through the undergrowth. Had his current situation been less desperate, he would have been more positively amused at the site.

With what seemed like an explosive buzzing sound burst into his ears, jacked up his adrenaline, and made his hands break out in a cold sweat. Rattlesnake. More specifically, a black-tailed rattlesnake, there, just beside the deer trail he was following at the base of some Apache plume. The viper had a greenish tinge on its smooth, scaled, rope-like body, and the last few inches of the end of its tail were solid black. Not the most deadly rattler in this part of the country—the Mojave had that distinction. But any snake bite could seal his fate in a tragic way in light of his situation.

He froze in his tracks and observed without motion the three-foot-plus long serpent as it clung to the shade of the shrubbery and eyed his every move, flicking its dark tongue in and out of its mouth in an effort to identify the potential predator through the sensory organs in its mouth. Ironic, really. He knew that he just might successfully evade helicopter and fixed-wing aircraft patrols, search dogs, search and rescue personnel, and other law enforcement technology out there. But a rattlesnake—something that cannot utter a single intelligible syllable—could disable or kill him with a single bite. It was perhaps less degrading than the pungy sticks the Viet Cong used in Viet Nam where they dug a shallow hole, embedded sharp wooden stakes sticking upward through human feces. Before metal plates were put in the soles of their jungle boots, a filthy deadly wound could occur to the unwary Marine or soldier who stepped on one of these traps.

No worries. A cool head prevails. Freeze in your tracks. Don't move Joe—don't move. Wait him out; eventually the serpent will relax, drop its guard; then you can back off and slip away unscathed. Now breathe in slowly; exhale slowly. Slowly. Slowwwwly. There now, you're breathing, you're living. No harm done. The snake lives, I live. Simple. *Crotalus molossus*—the scientific name for the black-tailed rattlesnake. Just passing through, Crotalus, just passing through.

Crotalus flicked his tongue in and out silently, trying to detect temperature variance in its surroundings. The serpent seemed like a living, breathing coiled spring—strong and ready to uncoil at any moment. Joe Mack recalled many a tale his Latino neighbors or

Native Americans told about the spirituality of the snakes and other animals. He pondered it a bit. Such a fascinating creature. Scary, but fascinating. No, there was nothing spiritual here—not unless it was demonic. This was a creature facilitated to survive on its belly in a harsh environment. It was equipped with wondrous sensory perception in its head and used its creepy tongue as an instrument of sorts to decipher what living things were in close proximity.

It seemed like a long while, but the snake did simply freeze in position if not relax. Its shiny black eyes were fixed on the object of concern—a man—Joe Mack. Ever so gently, ever so cautiously he backed away slowly, micro inches at a time. It was nothing to rush.

Joe Mack recalled a snake bite that Johnny O'Grady had gotten on his right calf muscle. The leg had swollen so bad that his skin cracked and discolored into shades of purple and red. He had been near death when Joe visited him in the hospital in Carlsbad those years ago, and he still had a sizable scar on that leg and a bit of a hitch in his gait when he walked.

God was indeed with him this day. He had stealthily backed off from the black-tailed rattlesnake and proceeded on to nowhere in particular. Ever aware of his situation, he paused and panned the landscape around him in a 360-degree scan. He was, after all, a fugitive. He must keep some space between himself and misinformed law enforcement officers who might pursue him more aggressively through a gun site than through investigation. He did not rape and murder poor Aubrey Flores. What was worse, he had a pretty good inclination of who had. Somehow, he must match the pieces of the puzzle together without any more incriminating scrapes with the law. Justice must be served. He must be made righteous in the eyes of his neighbors, the law, and almighty God. He must persevere—he would. He was, after all, a Marine. Once a Marine, always a Marine. He would stare death in the face and laugh. He would succeed—he must—for Cassie.

As he walked slowly among the ancient coniferous forest above the high Chihuahuan Desert, he meditated on Cassie. Did he really know her? Had he ever really known her? But then, if he did not, who did? There were secrets buried in her heart, in her mind, in her past—of that he was sure. True, she had hurt him—hurt him badly. But then, no one is more capable of hurting another person more effectively than the one who is closest. It made perfect sense. Perhaps the devil was to blame after all. Joe knew he was no unblemished prize himself. He would have to admit he was infatuated with screen actress Doris Day, which was silly of course. Worse yet, he had taken liberties with prostitutes in the Philippines and Viet Nam despite his Christian upbringing. The fact that he was concerned that he might die without having carnal knowledge of someone was hardly an excuse, but it was the only excuse he had. He thought about every aspect of this lovely blonde-haired blue-eyed girl that he loved. There was some unresolved hurt from her past that she had not divulged to him. Still, he loved her. He had every justification to find someone else, and certainly he had the opportunities. Yet, if he gave up on her—if heaven forbid he never so much as prayed for her—who would?

He paused for a moment noting that something appeared dark in the brush up ahead. At first he thought it a mere shadow, but upon closer inspection noted that there was a hole in rock going straight down God only knew how far. The Guadalupe Mountains were honey-combed limestone, of that there was no doubt. Hence, there had been many reports over the years of hidden gold and other loot stashed by robbers and prospectors alike. It was quite possible that he had accidentally stumbled upon a vertical shaft that led to an enormous cavern yet undiscovered. It might lead to cave formations more pristine, more wondrous than those in Carlsbad Caverns to the north of here. He picked up a small stone and dropped it into the black abyss. He strained his ear and listened carefully for what seemed like many seconds before he heard the report of the rock hitting on another surface far below. Suddenly, he got goose flesh at the thought of what unknown world he was perched on top of. What vast, cavernous wilderness lay just beneath him? Did it lead to a caver's dream world of speleothems and vast cave vistas? Had any human being ever stumbled upon this entrance, much less explored the subterranean expanse below? Or worse yet, was it a hidden entrance to the very pits of hell...

He meditated on the geologic anomaly for a while, then plucked a broad blade of grass from near the entrance. Cavers and geologists had often talked about wind currents at the entrance of caves. Joe Mack lowered his hand into the cavern entrance and let the blade of grass fall. Even before he let it go he discerned a slight updraft of air from the opening, cooling the clammy skin on the underneath of his arm. The blade of grass fluttered upward instead of making a steady spiraling descent into the underworld. It returned upward a few inches to the level of the ground where Joe stood, then a slight cross-wind on the surface blew it slightly away from the opening.

It could mean only one thing: There was another exposed entrance or exit to this uncharted cave, even though he could see no obvious light. Not far away the mountains dropped off abruptly into the South McKittrick Canyon drainage. Perhaps there was an opening out onto the southern canyon wall. Maybe, just maybe, he could enter at one point and exit another. It was worth a gamble, particularly if hounds were used to pick up his trail with a sheriff's posse or park rangers in tow. There was only one way to find out and his prospects of eluding his pursuers much longer were grim if he didn't have some sort of miraculous breakthrough.

Without further ado, he retrieved a coil of rope, some leather gloves, and a head lamp from his pack. To avoid any obvious detection, he tied it off slightly below the entrance onto the massive root from a pinyon pine tree.

Just as he was ready to descend, he noticed the shadowy figure of a mysterious man perhaps 60 yards away at the edge of a group of trees. The man—he strained his eyes—appeared to be an Apache from the days of old. The mysterious, barefoot Indian character wore a loin sash and cloth headband, and if Joe Mack wasn't mistaken—it appeared as though he had a wooden cross necklace, possibly hand carved. Suddenly he recollected the legend of John Seven-Oaks, an orphan who had been raised by a Mescalero Apache couple. His adopted parents had been senselessly murdered when John was nine years old—he had been shot in the throat and lived, though he would never utter a sound again. Was it possible? Could this be John Seven-Oaks?

The mysterious figure looked at him blankly, then raised his chin in the air as if in silent greeting. Joe Mack could swear that he saw a scar in the center of his throat. The man began gesturing as if wanting to communicate something, but obviously didn't want to come any nearer. He touched the scar on his throat with his index and middle fingers, then brought these fingers to his lips. He repeated this gesture a couple of times, then raised both arms up high and looked to the sky. Joe Mack was mesmerized by this stranger. The Apache character then pointed directly at Joe, then one more time up to the sky, as if trying to get Joe to look up. He did, and when he returned his gaze to where the Apache had been he discovered that he had simply melted into the forest, leaving Joe to wonder if he had ever really been there. Joe had heard old-timers tell tales of holdout Apache who continued to dwell on their own or in tiny bands rather than stay on the reservation. If Joe indeed saw who he thought he saw, Seven-Oaks had cut the heads off of his adopted parents' killers nearly ten years after their murder and was rumored to have raided the gardens and livestock of ranchers and settlers in the area around the Guadalupes. The legends he had heard went on to say how he had saved a young woman who had fallen off her horse and been snake bit, treating the bite and carrying her back to safety. If it was Seven-Oaks, he was perhaps a vision to Joe that eluding the law was within the realm of possibility—especially here in the Guadalupes. He had pointed skyward—to God perhaps?

Joe looked back at the ominous hole in the limestone reef he sat upon. He took a deep breath, turned on the headlamp which was strapped around his head, and with feet against the rock wall, started his descent into a possible subterranean hell.

Nearby, a red-tailed hawk eyed him curiously from atop an ancient dead snag of a Douglas fir tree. The noble bird cocked its head from side to side as it focused in on this peculiar creature. It watched as Joe Mack disappeared from sight like a faint wisp of smoke in the fierce West Texas wind...

CHAPTER 16

PORTRAIT OF A MONSTER

Salvador Quiones zipped up his jeans and wiped the sweat from his brow as he looked down at the lifeless body of the young woman he had just raped and murdered. Occasionally he thought what he was doing was very wrong, but he seemed incapable of stopping, and what was worse, he didn't want to stop.

Something tripped in his very brain; it was akin to a drug-induced high. He was just as hooked on his heinous crimes and victimization of women weaker than himself as a junkie was to LSD.

Salvador looked slowly and casually around his location with little worry. He had carefully picked out a remote location to do his dirty deed, and he had noted that there were no visible signs of humanity. So many places to torment, murder, and dispatch a person out in this vast Chihuahuan Desert. He retrieved a shovel from the back of his pickup truck and started to dig in a barren spot amid the greasewood brush. The somewhat pungent aroma of the creosote bush heating up in the midday sun was familiar to his senses. Equally familiar was him taking to the task of digging a shallow grave and nonchalantly disposing of someone's baby, someone's loved one. To Salvador, it was only wrong if he got caught—as long as he didn't get caught...

The girl was nineteen years, five months, and twenty-three days on this earth before she had the misfortune of hitching a ride with this monster who preyed on the unwary in this parched southwestern environment. Her name was Candice, "Candy" her friends had called her. Five minutes of perverted pleasure on his part would end an entire lifetime for this hapless girl. His only annoyance was that the dust was coating his ostrich-skin boots, soiling his meticulously clean and pressed blue jeans with light-colored dust.

He noted a nice looking horse crippler cactus near her grave, and he took care not to damage it. He mused how he had something in common with this plant with the savage-looking thorns—even if its name was somewhat erroneous. Salvador was a loner, and his thorns were perversion and cruelty, callousness and apathy to pleas for mercy. Worse yet, he derived a certain satisfaction at the teary-eyed looks of horror and despair and was aroused by their desperate pleas—even screams for mercy. In some remote sections of the desert, they might as well plea with this horse crippler cactus—for no human rescuer was anywhere close to within earshot.

He wasn't sure when he had first picked up the habit of throwing the first shovel full of dirt on the victim's face—perhaps it was the very first time. It was so much easier to finish the task once the face was hidden. Salvador was very superstitious. Even in death, perhaps the dead could see the villain who had put them in these unmarked graves. No, better to cover the face with dirt first, then the rest of the body could be covered.

As he had always done he threw the extra soil widely about so as to not make a mound that protruded noticeably. The body displaced a lot of the soil; that soil had to be scattered abroad. Once done he broke off a handful of creosote bush branches and feathered out the ground, brushing out his tracks all the way to his truck.

He smiled in amusement at the fact that the Federales had never caught up with him over the border, and not even the Texas Rangers had caught up with him here in Texas.

He was cunning and smooth and cold as a snake. He existed only to satiate his own desires and to evade capture and punishment.

Still, he reluctantly had to admit to himself that he had made a grievous error in raping and killing the young girl in her home. There were way too many means by which he could have been caught in that impulsive action. The victim's body was left to be examined. He may have left fingerprints, or tire tracks. There was nothing fruitful to be gained worrying about it now; ironically, he had caught a news clip that some poor, dumb gringo cowboy/ex-Marine was taking the rap for Salvador's work! If the Texas Rangers and Americano police reacted the way the Federales and Mexican police had—that cowboy would be shot to pieces before he ever had a chance to proclaim his innocence. Salvador Quionnes grinned a sardonic grin.

As he stepped back he heard the all too familiar terrifying sound of a rattle. Freezing in his tracks, he slowly turned his head in the direction of the sound and noted a diamondback rattlesnake coiled near his left leg. At a guess, he figured it was four to five feet long and as thick around as summer sausage. The snake flicked its tongue in and out of its shovel-shaped head rapidly, the demonic little eyes fixed in his direction. Salvador did a careful slide step to his right and the snake lunged but missed. Salvador fairly well trembled with laughter and admiration for this predator that dwelled in the dust.

"Aha, mi amigo! You are just like me—don't you think?" It was almost as though he expected the serpent to give him an audible reply.

"What's that my friend? You want the girl? You want a *piece of Candy*? There she is, you can have her, help yourself!" And he laughed manically again as he kicked some dirt in the direction of the shallow grave with his boot, immensely proud of himself for the little pun he had made in regard to her name. Then, clutching the shovel tightly he swirled around violently smashing downward onto the snake's head. He hit it repeatedly and excessively, violently out of control until he nearly broke the shovel handle. Finally, gasping for breath, he shouted,

"Cabron! I do not hate you for what you are, but you nearly bit me—your brother—and for that you must be punished!"

Salvador Quiones is a man—no, a monster—a demon. Stands 5' 9" tall, weighs 165 pounds. Likes his blue jeans starched and pressed and wears cowboy boots made from exotic skins. Although his main hobbies are rape and murder, he does also enjoy sports, bullfighting certainly, cock and dog fighting as well—especially to the death. Boxing is okay once in a while, especially if there is a bloody knockout or one of the pugilists happens to die from too many blows to the head.

Salvador loves a white straw cowboy hat. Like a snake or a lion or a scorpion or a spider—he is a predator. Killing is a means of covering his trail. Death to the tormented ensures that he continues to feed his perverted lusts without discovery. No one and no thing is sacred to Salvador Quiones. He and his brother had killed their father. The tears of his dearly departed mother would mean no more to him than a discarded newspaper blowing in the wind. It was all just so much trash. It was nothing. Nothing at all.

Yet, there were times when he slept. When he slept. When he slept—that the ghosts of those he had raped and murdered haunted him. Sometimes he woke up in a cold, terrified sweat. Demonic figures with reptilian features and amazingly horrific red eyes stared upon him and he knew he could find no escape. His ears were flooded with the indescribably tormented wails of unseen victims gnashing their teeth. In these dreams was utter despair and hopelessness, there was fear beyond description. He knew he would be destined to reside in the abyss of hell forever, tormented by the very demons he had emulated when was alive and well and walking upon the earth. Sadly, there was no turning back. No turning back. He was a depraved man. It would take luck or God and his angels to direct the path of someone to deal with this vile terror of the Chihuahuan Desert...

CHAPTER 17

CASSIE'S TEST

Cassie Mack brushed her hair in front of her bathroom mirror. Like any day, she would spend a significant amount of time in front of the mirror making sure her makeup, her hair everything was the best that it could be.

Joe Mack had teased her once about how women were better at applying camouflage than Marines preparing for jungle warfare. It was only once. Joe Mack, though he had his faults, could not be faulted for lacking in perception. He had perceived that Cassie's ritual of applying her makeup just so, and getting her hair perfect, was a ritual best left respected by an outsider. Besides, Joe was always pleased with the end result.

Cassie paused with her hair brush and smiled a little thinking about him. Damn, how he could flatter her like no one else could. Perhaps, after all, he truly loved her, like no one else would.

Be that as it may, she still seemed drawn to the much older and suave Texas Ranger, Whitmore. It was outrageous, of course. Still, there was something inside her she couldn't seem to shake. She noticed how his eyes assessed her in the restaurant interview, and she had discerned how he attempted to be nonchalant. Yet—on another note he didn't appear to mask his appreciation for a young woman he perceived to be so beautiful, so chipper and perky. She could not know of the trials and tribulations he had gone through with his alcoholic wife, a wife whose drinking led to the untimely, tragic death of their only son.

There would be much that Cassie would learn, however. Rest assured; the suave, handsome Ranger would pay her a visit again. Her pleasant smile for just a millisecond betrayed an almost sadistic sneer. This Whitmore might have status and even money, but many a man would crater to the beauty and charms of a simple maiden.

Suddenly, almost violently, she threw her hair brush at the mirror, actually cracking the glass. A solitary tear streamed down her cheek eroding an ever so faint, almost indiscernible furrow in her makeup. Her fantasies were once again leading her down a path where she knew she had been before, and where she should not dwell at all.

Almost to add insult to injury, there was something worse than an unexpected phone call—an unfamiliar knock at the door. Her heart immediately commenced pounding and there was a discernible trace of perspiration accumulating in the palms of her hands. There was a tightening in her throat and the sudden impulse to gasp. Another polite knock on the door. Cassie sucked in a deep breath, exhaled slowly, then as nonchalantly as she could asked, "Yes, who is it?"

"Miss Cassie, it's me, Percy Whitmore. Could I trouble you with a few more inquiries please?"

There was an uncomfortable period of silence and Whitmore pursued in explanation, "I have to be driving back to Van Horn and El Paso today, and there's something I wanted to approach you with. It will only take a minute."

Percy's tone was deep and smooth, mature, confident and reassuring. He sounded almost empathetic to her situation, like a loving father or doting uncle. If ever a voice could be compared to a fine, aged bourbon, or cognac, it was Percy Whitmore's voice.

Her heart beat with a different flutter now, and Cassie knew she was desirous of something she shouldn't pursue with this handsome Ranger, but somehow couldn't—or wouldn't—try to stop her impulses. After all, this was official business, and after all, wasn't it better that she be infatuated with a law enforcement professional than some oil field trash?

She applied her emotional brakes so as not to open the door in too much earnest or exhibit too much enthusiasm and excitement at greeting Percy.

Percy Whitmore heard the chain security latch being disconnected and the sound of Cassie turning the doorknob to allow him in.

Whitmore marveled at how he had a case of some giddy anxiety waiting for the door to open. For crying out loud, he was here on official law enforcement business, yet he was like a teenaged boy on a selfish mission to impress a pretty girl.

"Ranger Whitmore," she started with a peculiarly vulnerable expression on her face.

"Please, dispense with the formalities—Percy will do. I'm just a man doing his job and, if possible, I'd like to be your friend."

Cassie admired the meticulously trimmed and groomed salt-and-pepper hair and mustache of this West Texas lawman. The starched and pressed jeans, shiny polished roper-style cowboy boots, and white Stetson cowboy hat. This was a man who paid attention to detail, who made a point to be a gentleman, and put other people's needs above his own. At least on the surface. There was a kind of nobility about him, yet there was a lot to be said about age and treachery...

Percy looked about the room, somewhat sparsely furnished, yet neat and attractive. He noted a picture on a bureau of Cassie standing with a horse, head to head, smiling, with her cheek touching the horse on one side and her hand on the other. Another photo was a cowboy obviously breaking a horse.

"Nice pictures—care to share?" he inquired.

"That's me and Strawberry in the photo. Joe Mack named him."

"After the Marty Robbins song?"

"Yes," she laughed slightly, "after the Marty Robbins song. But he really wasn't such a notorious outlaw of a horse like the one in the song. He just liked the song I guess. The other photo is Joe breaking a horse—now that horse was more like the one in the song."

"Ah, so that's Joe Mack."

Percy knew the song, and the lyrics started playing in his mind as he studied the pictures trying to absorb every possibly detail.

"...Down in the horse corral, standin' alone Is an old Caballo, a Strawberry Roan His legs are all spavined, he's got pigeon toes, Little pig eyes and a big Roman nose.

... U-necked and old with a long, lower jaw I could see with one eye, he's a regular outlaw

I gets the blinds on 'im and it sure is a fright, Next comes the saddle and I screws it down tight Then I steps on 'im and I raises the blinds, Get out the way boys, he's gonna unwind

He sure is a frog-walker, he heaves a big sigh, He only lacks wings for to be on the fly, He turns his old belly right up to the sun, He sure is a sun-fishin', son-of-a-gun ..."

"Miss Cassie, I'd like to make you a proposal," he began, having taken off his Stetson and holding it in his hands.

"I'd like to help you. I'd like you to arrange a meeting with your husband, Joe Mack, to meet you somewhere, and let me know where that is and when."

"Oh, Percy," she gasped, "Don't you realize what you're asking? Can you ever look past a clinical pursuit of justice? Joe Mack is my husband—maybe, if he'll take me back."

Percy paused for a moment, realizing that he was unjustifiably jealous of Joe Mack and the love that was not yet extinguished with his estranged wife.

"Why sure he'll take you back, Miss Cassie, I'd bet every short-horn bull in Texas on that. What man would ever refuse a beautiful woman like you a second chance at anything?"

She meditated on that for a moment, and realized that there was more than a good chance that what he stated was true. Joe Mack had a heart of gold, and yet...

What happened next was almost inexplicable. Cassie looked up with tears in her eyes at the tall dark Texas Ranger. To Whitmore, her eyes were incomprehensibly beautiful, somewhat tragic and pathetic. He saw pain, confusion, insecurity, love, and deception—all in those magnificent eyes of blue.

He reached for her shoulders to give her a reassuring hug, and Cassie a little over zealously embraced him and squeezed him tight.

Percy could feel her hot tears soaking into his white Western shirt on his right breast, and he held her all the tighter. The damnable sin of it all was that he enjoyed the embrace and did not want it to end. He had not felt this sort of passion and excitement in his soul for quite some time, wrong though it might be.

The silence was not replaceable; they were at somewhat of a stand-off as to what to do next. He caressed her back with the palm of his hand in a soothing, comforting fashion. It was insanity. He welcomed her deep heaves for breath, fast blinks of the eyelids attempting to stifle confused tears, muting her impulsive, uncontrollable sobs. He kissed her affectionately on top of her head. Percy held her tighter, almost whispering in soft tones that everything would be alright. He massaged the tense muscles of her upper back while relishing the sensation of her soft breasts compressing into his chest.

Whether accident or conscious action, his massaging motion unhooked the fasteners on her bra and he felt the tension of the strap release. Cassie froze her motion and held her breath. How she responded now was critical, and there could be little turning back the course of events whichever way she chose. She must not repeat history, she must break the cycle, she must emerge victorious from her past! But it was so hard—she had such irresistible desires, and her flesh was so weak and her carnal desires so strong. What would she do? What should she do? What could she do?

Percy's heart was pounding so hard that he suspected Cassie could feel it as he pressed her near. He knew he was going down a path he should not go down, and yet he didn't care. He didn't want to stop; whatever it was felt too good. He had once heard a preacher say, "Sin is fun for a season, then..." Then. Then guilt, and shame and destruction. In rapid fire, almost newsreel fashion, Percy could see his career, his personal life, his reputation—all of them—going down in flames. This lovely young maiden was hard to resist—and yet—she was not his to indulge in. His sinful passion toward her could cloud his objectivity in the manhunt for her estranged husband, possibly jeopardize a most righteous outcome of events. Still, the euphoria of the moment persisted. The hot burning desire, the emotions burning out of control like a forest fire.

"Percy—no," Cassie whispered. She reached her hands behind her back and masterfully refastened her bra.

The simple statement and gesture deflated Percy. The dark side of him wanted to plead with her to reconsider—but he knew it was wrong.

Cassie's face was somewhat blushing, her expression troubled, psychologically unable to muster up her voice or put together any utterance of intelligent thought or expression of motivation for her actions.

It was quiet, and their embrace on each other relaxed, and they could not bear to look directly upon one another.

If one believed in things spiritual in nature, or of resisting a spirit of lust—Cassie had passed the test. As for Percival Pinkerton Whitmore...

CHAPTER 18

A Time To Heal

"Mr. Whitmore..."

"Yes, Miss Cassie?" he asked with a worried expression.

"That must never happen again; I'm trying, I need..."

"No need to explain, I'm terribly sorry, I, I just...," his voice faded, searching for the right words to say. He looked around the apartment and seemed to inquire with his facial gesture whether or not it was okay to sit on the couch. Cassie nodded in reply and motioned with her hand in acknowledgment. Percy sat on one end of the couch nervously fidgeting with his Stetson. He knew all too well that they had come close to something more intimate on the couch than a conversation about his painful past.

"If I might ask, Percy, what is the story with, uh, with your wife?"

Like a stunned steer in the slaughter house, Percival Pinkerton Whitmore just sat there for a moment dazed. He was supposed to be the one here asking the questions—business questions. This young woman was not just some naive beauty. She had insight, she was reading his mail now. She knew men. Yet, somehow it seemed sincere, and for reasons that God only knew, he somehow felt resigned to open up to her in honesty.

"Well, she's a good woman with a bad drinking problem. Just something that's built up over the years and taken a mighty toll in recent times. I didn't realize I was so transparent, such an obvious depiction of an older man in mid-life crisis..."

"I didn't mean you harm, Mr. Whitmore. I would never take you to be whimsical or foolish, impulsive or ungentleman-like. You are a handsome man and a gentleman. Do you have any children?"

"We had a boy—a really fine, goodhearted, humorous son. He was more into baseball than being a cowboy. I think he would have gone real far in life..."

"I'm sorry, what happened?"

"Helen had been drinking heavily and was driving him home from a baseball game, actually. I was working a case and closing in on solving a crime that night and couldn't make the game. It seems like I could rarely ever make a game..."

Percy's eyes began to water and the grief and remorse in them betrayed a gentler self than he cared to project.

"Her state of intoxication impaired her judgment and she drove through a red light at an intersection. Travis' side of the car was hit directly, he, he..."

"I am so sorry—I shouldn't have asked."

"No, it's alright. God knows I certainly pushed the envelope in a shameful way just moments ago. I reckon I owe you this much."

"It's alright, really. Please, do go on."

"Well, as you might imagine, it is quite difficult for me to talk about. It is quite difficult for us to deal with on the home front even now. It's surreal; it's hard to sort out, to comprehend the pain, the loss. These days we could've lost him in Viet Nam or something, but a senseless car wreck..."

"And your wife?"

"Helen. Her name is Helen. She blames herself of course—she has never stopped hurting. She's tried to kill herself several times. I've threatened to leave her, and she's begged me to do so. She had an affair for a while, but I know it was only an attempt to get me out of her life, a vain attempt to erase the memories..."

"It seems no one has a bed of roses to lie on these days—everyone has their cross to bear, their burdens which are unseen, or unknown to most," Cassie mused aloud.

For a while, there was just silence. There were only fixed stares into a void. Quiet. Still. Contemplative.

Cassie reached to turn the knob on the radio in an uncomfortable bid to break the silence and change the solemn atmosphere. Even that act resulted in the unexpected as the next song on the radio seemed to minister to the situation. Ironically, it was a song by the Birds titled, *Turn, Turn, Turn.* How fitting; the lyrics, for the most part Percy recognized, came from the Bible, specifically from the Book of Ecclesiastes:

To everything there is a season, and a time to every purpose under the heaven:

A time to be born, and a time to die; a time to plant, a time to reap that which is planted;

A time to kill, and a time to heal; a time to break down, and a time to build up;

A time to weep, and a time to laugh; a time to mourn, and a time to dance;

A time to cast away stones, and a time to gather stones together; a time to embrace, and a time to refrain from embracing;

A time to get, and a time to lose; a time to keep, and a time to cast away;

A time to rend, and a time to sew; a time to keep silence, and a time to speak;

A time to love, and a time to hate; a time of war, and a time of peace.

They sat there in the tiny living room of the apartment, mesmerized by the lyrics. Tears flowed softly and steadily down their cheeks. It was an upheaval of emotions, it was a time of cleansing the spirit.

Now it was Cassie who sat down softly beside Percy and gave him a comforting hug on the shoulder. It was as though a light switch had been turned on and both of them saw things in a different light, if only for the moment. For that moment, it was just an innocent friendship—two tortured souls being vulnerable to one another. Percy seemed more fatherly now, and to Percy, she now appeared more like a cherished daughter. It was one of the few times since the tragic death of his son that the valiant Texas Ranger sobbed, though it was somewhat stifled. He no longer cared to bury the pain, to hide his remorse, to put up a facade of strength. He was, after all, just a man.

CHAPTER 19

The Descent into South McKittrick

Joe Mack wedged himself slowly downward in the limestone shaft toward a vague glimmer of light. He knew not what he was getting himself into—there could be a bottomless chasm just beneath him that would swallow him up forever—never to be found—should he slip. Then again, there could be a den or rattlesnakes or poisonous gasses associated with caves. All of these things were common concerns in this part of the country.

Clutching the rope tightly, he inched his way down. The air was cooler in this hidden shaft in the rock, and it smelled of somewhat damp limestone. Upon further inspection with his headlamp, a hole did indeed proceed on to depths unknown, his light not penetrating far enough to see the bottom. But to the canyon side a shaft of light was clearly visible; years of water erosion had provided an exit onto one of the ancient limestone cliff faces that enclosed the South McKittrick Canyon drainage.

At first glimpse, he felt utter despair at the height at which he was, doubting that he had enough rope to descend safely to the bottom. An instant surge of panic gripped him, but he quickly checked himself, muttering aloud that panic could be his worst enemy right now. He sucked in his breath slowly and exhaled slowly. It was like taking the shot.

B.R.A.S.S. Breathe. Relax. Aim. Stop. Squeeze. He looked out the opening, clutching tightly to the jagged limestone opening lest he fall. At worst, he would have to re-ascend the shaft and get back on top of the ridge and go to plan B. He didn't want plan B; however, should dogs be used to track him, this would be a most excellent distraction.

The exit onto the cliff face of South McKittrick was in essence a cave opening, and he was crouching in it. To the casual observer down below, it would be barely discernible. The forces of water, wind, and erosion over thousands of years had etched a shallow trough which started straight down, then veered off to his left a little before disappearing. From that point a small cliff ledge was accessible which had vegetation on it a small ponderosa pine and some mountain mahogany, sotol, and grass. From that point he would just have to scope it out as it was a cinch he did not have enough rope to descend to the canyon floor from here. The further down, perhaps the greater the possibility. Then again, he might just free climb and not use rope at all. Certainly he would start that way.

With his face outward from the cliff face, he sprawled like a spider in reverse, wedging himself with his hands and feet and inching his way downward. A cool sweat broke out on his forehead—he had a thing about heights—didn't like them too much! It wasn't the current environment so much as the thought of a slip or fall and sudden, deadly stop at the bottom. That must not happen. Not with possibilities on the horizon with him and Cassie. There were so many seemingly insurmountable obstacles to patching up his marriage. Perhaps if he made this climb, he would simply end up in a dreadful prison for the next twenty years. Perhaps he would be shot on sight and never even make it to his day in court.

"Mister, you better just concentrate on getting down off this mountain right now," he muttered to himself between clinched teeth.

He succeeded in spider-crawling down the straight, which now veered off to the left. To his relief, there was a little more of a shelf to it than appeared to be the case from the cave entrance.

"Thank you, Lord!" he gasped aloud, steadfastly heading toward the vegetated cliff, which was down to his left and somewhat lower.

It was a pristinely sunny day with a blue sky and few clouds, which only occasionally diffused the sunlight. The view of the canyon was spectacular from this vantage point with an intermittent, meandering stream of crystal clear water flowing among the rocks. He could see travertine dams in places where the calcium carbonate had solidified making natural little pools along the stream. They were shaped somewhat like large lily pads from a more tropical environment. The sight was just inconceivably beautiful, even to a man on the run, even to a man who had grown up in the shadow of these mountains and explored their vast regions.

Stepping onto the vegetated ledge, he exhaled a gasp of relief. He felt he was on safer footing, at least for the moment, until he could size up his situation. He studied the ground not only for sound footing but also for the ever-present possibility of happening upon a rattlesnake. It was in the fall of the year now; they would still be active for a while and a most unwelcome surprise right now. Nothing. Nothing but the plants and rocks he had observed from above. If need be, there was a small ponderosa pine he could secure his rope to which would hold his weight. He would rather not have to leave a significant piece of evidence such as that, but if need be he would.

Further along, the ledge went to the west, up canyon, and toward a talus slope that could be traversed, it appeared, all the way to the canyon floor. Between the ledge and the talus was a small area that appeared to be smoother rock and quite perilous to cross en route to the talus slope.

Joe Mack's heart was pounding rapidly, not so much from the physical exertion as from the fear of sliding or falling at some point. The Guadalupes often hid drop-offs until you were right upon them, leaving a person "cliffed out" they called it, sometimes having to backtrack over a lot of ground in search of an easier descent. That's why, where possible, one stuck to established trails, trails made either by man or by deer, sheep, and cattle over the years.

He had walked the short distance to the end of his safe, vegetated cliff sanctuary with its spectacular view of South McKittrick Canyon and the impressive McKittrick Ridge across from him. The rock face was intimidating to say the least. One slip and there would be no stopping a deadly slide to the canyon floor. There were some cracks and rough areas on the otherwise smooth face that he could hang onto to inch his way along. The rope would actually be of no use at this point as it still wouldn't be long enough to get him to the bottom. Joe Mack softly muttered a prayer aloud as he clung to the rock face, this time face down with his body sucked up to the rock like a leech. There was a bit of slope to it, but it was far too steep if he lost a foot or handhold. He worried about the weight of his small back causing loss of balance, but it would be cumbersome to try to take it off now. He sucked in and inched his way along. He was in the shade of the cliff, but the sun glared not far away and was intense on the opposite limestone walls of the South McKittrick drainage. For some fleeting moments, he flashed back to the heat of Viet Nam, flat to the ground and motionless as a Viet Cong patrol walked by cautiously, unaware of the presence of him and the others in his squad.

"Focus, Joe, focus!" he hissed aloud.

"Now watch what you're doing, don't daydream!" he went on to scold himself.

This was no time for a slipup or miscalculation. At worst, if he could make it just a few more feet, then, even if he did slip it was a short distance to the boulders of the talus slope that would stop him—provided he didn't start a deadly rock slide. There were no good options, only limited ones—and hope. The song by Barry McGuire came into his mind, almost audible in his ears as if to emphasize the gravity of the situation:

"Don't you understand what I'm tryin' to say
Can't you feel the fears I'm feelin' today?
If the button is pushed, there's no runnin' away
There'll be no one to save, with the world in a grave
[Take a look around ya boy, it's bound to scare ya boy]

And you tell me
Over and over and over again, my friend
Ah, you don't believe
We're on the eve
of destruction."

Take a look around you boy, it's bound to scare you boy, take a look around you boy, it's bound to scare you boy! Ah, you don't believe, you're on the eve of destruction?"

"Stop it! Stop it!" he was nearly shouting now.

"Marine, you will get back in the saddle now, do you hear me boy?!"

"Sir, yes sir!" Joe answered himself fighting off panic.

One more hold—as he wedged his bleeding fingers deep into a crack. He inched over perhaps eight more inches toward safety. Then another foot. Five inches. Made it. Made it. On the rocks, thank God Almighty, he was finally on the rocks of the talus slope!

Quickly he scooted his body into the slope, but had to ease up just as quickly when rocks started to slide.

Like a jackhammer, his heart was pounding in his throat as he gasped for air and forced himself to gain his composure. The sliding rock subsided. When it was complete, he stealthily walked toward safer terrain, where should he slide there might be some vegetation to grab. Should a posse be up above even as he descended, a bunch of noise would ruin the whole advantage he had risked his life to achieve.

It was no time until he was out of the talus slope and working his way toward the canyon floor where he could rest 'neath the shade of trees and enjoy cool spring water while he de-escalated his emotions. It was in view now, and how beautiful it was! Less than a hundred yards to easy travel! Then it appeared—he was cliffed out. He stood on the edge of a cliff that dropped another thirty feet to one last gradual piece of slope to the canyon floor. The only problem was he had at best a twenty-foot length of rope in his backpack. So close, yet so far away.

CHAPTER 20

Charlie's Quest

Charlie Knox sat in his car with his binoculars watching Percival Pinkerton Whitmore exit Cassie Mack's apartment. He had been scoping it out to see if any other men, or better yet—Joe Mack—might have paid her a visit. Charlie squinted through the

binoculars as he observed what appeared to be a distraught Texas Ranger wiping his bloodshot eyes and then the bottom of his nose—as if, well as if quite frankly, he had been crying.

Knox slipped out the pint of Old Crow whiskey he had stashed in his glove box and took a pull in bewilderment.

" Hell, it's surely five o'clock somewhere," he muttered to himself.

He was into his second fifth of the day, and this was his fifty-seventh and a half cigarette. He was cutting back, difficult though it was.

"What the hell is going...," he stopped himself. Surely Percy Whitmore wouldn't try something like making unwelcome advances on that pretty little filly—or would he? Knox detested himself for even thinking such thoughts, but then the prevalence of such thoughts was somewhat inevitable in his profession.

Charlie Knox mused how he had come across a lot of scum in his lifetime in every shade and hue imaginable. White trash, black trash, brown trash, even a little red and yellow trash. Sort of like a rainbow, he thought—only trashy. Without scruples, without a moral compass or a shred of compassion or conscience. Hell, he was no bigot, his ex-wife was part Mescalero Apache, Hispanic, and gringo—the best of three worlds.

Charlie reflected back on Lydia—she was a beauty when he met her in his younger days. He was stronger then, slimmer, more hair, more energy and wit. He had prospered for a while, even had a few bucks left over in those days. But Lydia had skeletons in her own closet that she couldn't quite bury and leave dead. Every now and then, those old bones would be dug up and infest the hormone pool and the fight was on. Perhaps no one ever totally healed from physical and sexual abuse encountered in their youth, Charlie decided resignedly, but damn it, it wasn't his fault. He had worshiped the lady, and if he'd anywhere had the wherewithal he would have indeed roped the moon for Lydia. The intimate part of the marriage was strained every time it was time for bed, and quite often she would feign sleep. It was all the more reason why he was devastated when he found out she was having a fling with some railroad employee down from Albuquerque. The son of a gun definitely had more money than Charlie, and he had to admit, was a damn sight better looking. Still, the affair didn't last long after she left. No doubt the old boy encountered some of those frightening skeletons from Lydia's past and decided he had best get out of Dodge.

Charlie had begged her to take him back and work on their marriage—that he forgave her and would try to be everything that she wanted him to be.

He stared blankly at the front door to Cassie's apartment building and took another pull of Old Crow in a too well rehearsed methodical movement.

The problem with Lydia was that there could be no perfect man. She was void of trust and unhealed emotionally after nearly twenty years. Years ago, he had heard that she had taken some job in a strip joint in some sleazy Albuquerque rat nest. He had actually gotten the nerve up to case the joint once. He saw her going in to work in the late afternoon with an expression that conveyed both hardness and despair. It was as if he were paralyzed and literally could not lift the latch to open his car door and go inside. He recalled the feeling of nausea and breaking out in a cold sweat. He recalled the lead suit. Lead suit. Depression, sadness, heartbreak, and despair. No appetite. Barely able to lift his arms, take a breath, or walk to the bathroom. Little sleep, or too much sleep. He had lost nearly thirty pounds that he didn't have to lose back in those days before he decided to get back in the saddle and ride. From that day forward, he never tried to find her or contact her. Everything that his simple but well-intended spirit had thought wise to say had already been said. She was gone, gone, pure and simple. Nevertheless, he still cared.

The front door of Cassie's apartment building opened and out she came, obviously dressed in her uniform for work. Or was she? Charlie had a suspicion this little filly was a little wilier than he initially assumed, and she might just be putting on a show to keep him off her trail. He would follow her—perhaps this was just a tactic to keep spies such as himself off her trail and her real mission at hand.

Charlie slouched down in the car seat and held up a roadmap to hide his face. From what he could tell, she didn't even notice him. It was almost too easy. She walked to the Chevrolet Bel Aire and got inside. She looked mighty fine with those dark sunglasses, kind of Hollywood-like. She looked even better without them, he decided; those pretty blue eyes should never be covered except in dire emergency.

Knox capped the bottle of Old Crow and started his car, slowly and deliberately following Cassie Mack at a respectable distance. Right turn signal, then a left at the next block. The street did sort of an S shape through a neighborhood and still she proceeded onward at normal speed. Red brake lights, a turn signal to the left. What? What is going on? A church? She was stopped at a little Baptist church where two other cars were already parked in the small lot. Likely they belonged to the pastor, and perhaps the accountant. Always had to have someone manage the mammon, Charlie figured. He didn't have much use for most preachers because most preachers looked down their noses at the likes of him. He didn't need that kind of action, especially not from some Bible thumper acting holier than thou.

Cassie got out of the car, looking around a bit nervously before going into a side door of the church. Perhaps it led into the office. Certainly he wouldn't know, his abused, haggard old carcass hadn't darkened the door of a church since one of his colleague's funeral five years ago. Ben Salinas, a good cop and even better friend. Friends were something in very short supply in Charlie's world. In fact, he wasn't really sure if there was anyone left anymore that merited the honor of that title. A friend is something sacred, cherished, honored.

Friends would give you the shirt off their back when the chips were down. He gazed up at the steep pitched roof and the stained-glass windows. In fact, he seemed to recall, that the Bible had something to say about there being "no greater love than a man would lay down his life for a friend." Ben Salinas was that caliber of friend. Ben would go that far. Ben did go that far.

Charlie fumbled in the glove box for the nearly empty bottle of whiskey. Without looking at it, he unscrewed the cap while gazing out blankly at the stately architecture of the church and the beautifully manicured ground surrounding it. It wasn't a huge lawn, but then, this was Roswell, New Mexico. Water was perhaps more precious than silver in this part of the world, on the fringe of the Chihuahuan Desert.

Charlie mused at what Cassie Mack would be doing in a church in the middle of the week. He had never noticed her going there before. Perhaps it was a trick; perhaps she this was a rendezvous with her estranged husband Joe.

"God, I wish they would rendezvous for more than one reason." Charlie felt sorry for those two kids. Kids—he was certainly old enough to be their daddy. Charlie and Lydia never had any children, sex was something very uncomfortable with Lydia, but he hoped not on his regard. He daydreamed about those torturous days wondering what he might have done differently. Once she had that look about her to where he thought she might be pregnant. He had, in fact, asked her point-blank. Charlie wanted kids, he would like to have had a whole bushel of them, and he wasn't even Catholic. She only frowned at him like he was foolish for asking and told him, "Of course not—don't you think I would know?"

Be that as it may, a week later she took off on him—again, and this time was gone for three days. When she returned, there was a vacant look on her face, and what little warmth and cheer had been in her before seemed to have vanished forever. A part of her was missing that never seemed to come back. And somehow, with no verbal confirmation or tangible proof, Charlie felt as though a part of him had died that day as well, as if the one and only chance of his having a living breathing legacy to continue on after his demise had been taken away without a chance.

A short time later, Cassie came out of the church, seemingly in no big hurry. She appeared to be looking around to see if anyone noticed her, but once again didn't appear to notice Charlie.

Although not very spiritual, Charlie begged God's forgiveness for admiring Cassie's rather well-proportioned posterior a bit too long, and especially in the vicinity of a church. He had many regrets, disappointments in life, but for once his purpose and his quest were clear: He had to help clear Joe Mack's name, find the real killer, and bring these two young people back together where they belonged. Many a man would like to lay claim to her, but no other man had a right to in Charlie's mind.

Knox knew all too well the agony of loneliness, the depression one feels in an apartment by yourself night after night. He had tried the bar scene and failed miserably

at that as well. If you meet them in a bar, that's probably where you'll leave them some sad day.

Suddenly an idea came to Charlie. He would not follow Cassie, but rather go have a visit with whoever was inside that church. After all, it was a sunny day, no clouds overhead, so the fear of lightning striking him down before his sinful soul could clear the front door was somewhat diminished.

Charlie fished a comb out of his back pocket and made an honest effort to groom his greasy black hair and adjust his necktie. Optimistic about his revelation, he proceeded with renewed confidence to the side door that Cassie had used and knocked. When no one responded, he opened the door and went inside. Immediately, he heard the sound of a vacuum cleaner in the sanctuary of the church and spotted someone with his back to him dutifully cleaning the place.

"Uh, excuse me. Excuse me! Sir, hello, sir, could I have a moment?" Finally, he had spoken loudly enough and flailed his arms around in a somewhat comical fashion long enough to get the man's attention.

The man was a rather large sort, wearing sweat pants, a T-shirt, and white running shoes looked like he could take care of himself in a brawl if he had to. Knox figured he must be as big as that actor, John Wayne, and maybe just as tough. Must be the janitor or something Knox assumed.

"Excuse me, sir, I'm Charlie Knox, I'm a private investigator."

Somewhat to his amusement, the big gent flashed a beaming warm smile and extended a huge right hand to shake Charlie's warmly.

"I'm Pastor Jack Schafer. This is my little church. What can I do for you, son?"

Son? Charlie hadn't been bestowed that term in quite a few years, although he suspected the pastor might have a few years on him. Frankly, he kind of appreciated it.

"Well, you see I'm trying to help these two young kids who have one hell er, uh one heck of a mess on their hands. Fact is, Padre, I think you just got done talking to the young lady a few moments ago."

"Please, just call me Jack. So you're trying to help Cassie Mack, are you?"

"Well, as a matter of fact, yes Pa—er, I mean Jack. You know, funny thing, it just hit me I might try to semi-retire after this case. This case is sort of personal to me for some reason. Maybe I'd just like to see that couple end up with something better than I ended up with in life—know what I mean?"

Pastor Jack put one massive hand on Charlie's shoulder and stared into his eyes with a knowing look. After an uncomfortable pause, he injected, "Well, I don't really know you, Charlie, why don't we sit down in my office and talk about it? You probably walked right by it when you came in the side door."

"How did you know I used the side door?"

"Could be divine revelation, Charlie, but also, the front doors are locked!" he smiled.

They sat down and discussed the situation, and Charlie learned that Cassie had confided in this big fatherly figure in pretty great detail—right down to the affair she had had with the rig hand out of Hobbs, New Mexico. Charlie talked about a lot of things as the sun sank lower and lower in the southwestern sky. He divulged how women like Lydia, and Cassie, and, yes, little Aubrey were all someone's precious little babies—until the day they died and forever more. Granted, some children come into this world very wanted and with a great deal of joy and anticipation, while others often due to sinful circumstances came into this world of parents filled with fear and trepidation, immature minds, and selfish hearts. He ranted on how patrons of strip joints and houses of ill repute and porno films should be shamed with such realization. But, it was, alas, a very cruel and wicked world. Somewhat ironically, they mostly talked about Charlie.

It was probably an hour or more later that Charlie came walking out of that church with a King James Bible in his hand and a smile on his face. He had given his heart to Jesus that day and for the first time in years felt some level of peace and hope in his life. Pastor Jack had invited him to church on Sunday morning and Charlie's intentions were to go. Why not? What did he have to lose? He had certainly tried every other worldly thing there was; God appeared to be his last hope at turning things around in his miserable life.

He loosened his tie when he got in the car and fished out the bottle in the glove box. Although it was nearly empty, he dumped what was left out his window and started to pitch the bottle. No—better to throw it away properly someplace he thought.

As he drove off he hadn't noticed that Pastor Jack had been watching him the whole time from inside the church. He had a grin on his face as big as West Texas...

CHAPTER 21

Village of the Dead

Joe Mack had known early on that he had minimal rope to negotiate the mountains. He had let the length of it fall and figured he was ten to fifteen feet short. Damn, not much for options that wouldn't be either life threatening or arduous, or perhaps set him up to backtrack toward his pursuers. He studied the terrain beneath the rope. No problem in the regard that there were some sotol plants he could possibly land on and twist an ankle. The small barbs on their leaves would have no dire consequence. In his mind he knew he was simply going to have to get as low as he could, drop free, and land smart. The bad news was that he would have to leave the rope where it might be discovered.

He removed his pack and carefully tossed it into the thick mat of sotol plants the approximately thirty plus feet down below, kept his rifle slung on his back, then tied off his rope on a small alligator juniper tree. The trees were named such due to their rough bark, which resembled an alligator's scaly skin. He sucked in a deep breath, muttered a little prayer aloud, and descended, able to sort of walk down the cliff face with his feet, the front of his body facing the cliff. He got as low as he could get on the rope and scanned the ground below to scope out his landing. Fortunately there were no large agave plants or jagged rock. The weight of the pack off his back would lighten his impact a little.

He turned the balls of his feet downward and prepared to drop and roll like a parachutist does to lessen the impact. Joe had not been to airborne school, but had talked to others who had, so he had a good idea how to land. Besides, he had repelled out of helicopters and taken as much of a drop as he would take here. He let go.

The impact of the fall surprised him somehow, and he rolled backward to the point of doing a somersault. He got a few scratches but his rifle was fine and he was fine. Hopefully, there weren't trackers up above to have heard any sound. Hopefully, he wouldn't encounter any hikers, geologists, or park employees in the canyon who might be able to identify him or report on his whereabouts. Conceivably, his rope might never be found as this section of the canyon was rarely accessed by anyone.

Joe Mack breathed a sigh of relief and took in his surroundings without running around in a panic like a wild man. Should he have trackers on his trail, he should not tarry long. Had they any inkling he went into the canyon, they would simply go around the easy way by road and set up a perimeter for him to walk into. The canyon drainages were rugged, however, and there were a number of routes he could take. He could cut back up McKittrick Ridge up into the high country and work his way into the Lincoln National Forest. He could go up Middle McKittrick or North McKittrick. He must leave no more sign that a butterfly does for a trail, and he must not tarry too long in any one place.

He mused back about his surroundings; what a beautiful area, a refuge. What he would give if he could just be here forever and be left alone—he and his beautiful wife Cassie. He touched at the letter she had sent him buttoned up in his shirt pocket in a plastic bag. It was in some ways his most valuable possession right now.

Something very bizarre and tragic had happened in this canyon many years ago when the U.S. Cavalry was on patrol in search of Apache. It was in 1851, well before the Civil War, when young Lieutenant Richard Irving Dodge led a patrol into this very area and documented his journey well. An advance scout had traveled ahead in the canyon paradise and when he returned reporting a Mescalero village, Dodge ordered his troops to load up and prepare for attack. It was then that he was informed that all the Indians in the camp were mysteriously dead. In fact, thirty-five were dead and of mysterious causes. It was as though an angel of death had come into that camp and left by the wind. There was no evidence of the means of their death. The whole band was scattered in various locations about the camp, perhaps cleaning weapons or tending to a cooking fire. The teepees and shelters were in various stages of decay and disrepair when the cavalry troopers looked upon them in shocked amazement. They had never seen anything like it; nor likely had any detachment. It was but one of hundreds of stories and legends associated with the Guadalupe Mountains.

The thought of such occurrences raised goose flesh on Joe Mack's back; it gave him the creeps quite literally. One thing was for certain, a lot of things happen in this world that there's no logical explanation for.

Joe hated the thought of being naive or gullible, but the fact was he was gullible at times. He had believed in jackalopes for the longest time having seen the taxidermy jackrabbit head with small deer antlers affixed that looked authentic to him. He had learned through embarrassment to check out the facts for himself before relaying sensational stories. He had checked out the story of the Village of the Dead through historical records at Fort Davis National Historic Site south of the Guadalupes about 120 miles.

Joe looked up intensely at the ridge line through a thin veil of maple trees in this canyon oasis. There was for the moment no need to rush in case he should miss seeing any human activity whatsoever up along the ridgeline. He listened for the sounds of bloodhound search dogs or men's voices. Only silence interrupted periodically by various song birds or the screech of a patrolling red-tailed hawk gliding along high near the ridgelines looking for game below.

Joe sat with his legs crossed Indian style on a smooth, cool slab of limestone, wishing he could be that hawk if only for a day. He could fly to Cassie in the world's greatest disguise, hold her, and talk to her with no one knowing; hopefully, get her back into his life—back home. He closed his eyes for a moment and imagined the warmth of her body held close to his, the feel of her hair as he caressed it, and the subtle, pretty smell of her perfume. He fantasized about looking into those beautiful blue eyes as he had done so many, many times trying to decipher the mystery that she had buried within. She had built up walls in her life and he had earnestly worked to tear them down so that they might be more of one accord.

Those blue eyes, those beautiful blue eyes. He remembered the teary, angry eyes the day she had packed her things and told him she didn't love him anymore. He had sensed something wrong for some time but seemed powerless to do anything about it. He sat there recalling the song, *Blue Eyes Crying in the Rain,* sung by Hank Williams, and quite frankly some good local talent. Softly he sang the words,

"In the twilight glow I see her
Blue eyes crying in rain
When we kissed goodbye and parted
I knew we'd never meet again
Love is like a dying ember
And only memories remain
And through the ages I'll remember
Blue eyes crying in rain
Someday when we meet up yonder
We'll stroll hand in hand again
In the land that knows no parting
Blue eyes crying in rain."

Right now, it was his blue eyes that were crying as the tears streamed down his cheeks. Under the beautiful, sunny West Texas sky he was crying and brokenhearted.

"I miss you, Cassie, God how I miss you..."

Joe Mack buried his face in his folded arms for a while and wept until he regained his composure. His mind was always busy, it seemed; whether times were bad or good didn't matter. He eventually controlled his breath and regained his focus on the mission at hand.

"Dear God, it is so beautiful in here—this is paradise!" Joe sort of whispered aloud. Leaves on the maple trees were turning all different colors or red, orange, and yellow. The Texas madrone trees had bark as smooth and beautiful as the prettiest legs you've ever seen. Some would think it strange to revere these smooth-barked trees in somewhat of a sensuous vein, yet they were so incomprehensibly smooth and beautiful. With the unfortunate yet inevitable increased traffic with tourists, on rare occasions someone just had to carve their initials into the pristine, smooth, perfect bark. To Joe Mack, it was as senseless as a beautiful woman with a peaches-and-cream complexion getting a tattoo. To the artist, perhaps it was an empty palette, but to him, it could only defile what God had already made perfect. The trees had red berries and waxen-looking green leaves. Botanists claimed that they were actually a rainforest tree, and that these trees were a carryover from a wetter time. Joe marveled at the diversity of plants and animals, and the beautifully rugged geology that filled this canyon environment. He certainly wished he could linger—maybe someday when some level of sanity was restored to his life. Right now, unfortunately, he must push on.

CHAPTER 22

Hot Pursuit

Percival Pinkerton Whitmore was tall in the saddle riding with the sheriff's posse members up toward Pine Top on a more than good hunch that Joe Mack was on foot in the Guadalupes like a wily Apache trying to dodge his pursuers. Furthermore, they had an expert tracker and lion hunter with his three best hounds leading the way. Arlo McIntyre was legend in this part of the great Southwest, and the advocate of cattlemen and sheepmen alike in the pursuit of feline predators that ravaged their herds and flocks.

McIntyre was a burly man, dark skinned with a thick dark moustache and matching curly hair. His imposing six foot three inch, 230-pound mass mixed with an almost perpetual scowl on his face would be unnerving to most men, and to mountain lions, black bears, and even the occasional jaguar he and his hounds were almost always a death sentence. Neither was it his first rodeo in tracking fugitive men, and it was perhaps happenchance that they for the most part didn't seem to get taken alive either. Besides McIntyre and Whitmore, there were four other sheriff's posse members on the manhunt.

Trooper Jim Conklin limped up to the group at the trailhead, primarily chatting with Percy Whitmore.

"Remember, Percy, I'm counting on you to watch out for trigger itch out there. I still stand by my suspicions that I shared with you in the Van Horn hospital a while back," Conklin said sternly.

"No animosity about the hitch you have in that leg? Remember who gave it to you, don't you?" Whitmore replied in an amused tone with one eyebrow lifted high to further communicate skepticism.

"He didn't give me anything. I earned it in the line of duty. I still contend he didn't mean to hit me or anyone else with that slug. You forget, Percy, I know that boy. No one better be bringing him back draped over a saddle in my territory. He's a veteran for crying out loud; survived Viet Nam, and for what? This? Don't forget he's a Marine like you—don't you boys have a code you live by?"

Percy felt the barb from that last one. Of course, there was a code. Once a Marine always a Marine. Semper Fidelis. Marines look out for each other. And, to almost no one's knowledge, there was the embarrassing little episode with Cassie Mack, which he prayed to God never became knowledge to anyone else; if it had gone a step further it would have been even more disastrous.

"I'm reading you loud and clear, Jimbo. It's your leg anyhow. We'll chat about it over a cup of coffee at the Pine Springs Café when we bring him in. And I have a strong hunch we will bring him in." Then, after a short pause, "Alive."

Percy looked beyond Conklin and saw what appeared to be a television news crew pulling up. "Adios" to them he thought, he didn't have the stomach for a bunch of journalists coming in to mess up the truth of a story. Conklin and the Parkies could deal with them as far as he was concerned.

Arlo McIntyre held an article of Joe Mack's clothing to the hounds' noses then put it back in his saddlebag. The dogs were hyper and wagging their tails. Arlo checked the cinch of the saddle on his mount, then hoisted his heavy frame up onto the poor horse that would have to carry him several thousand feet up the mountain, and perhaps do that time and again depending on whether they picked up his trail, and where it led them.

Percy noted the uniform coat of almost white dust covering his otherwise well-shined roper boots and resisted the urge to wipe them off. He was in the saddle now, and there was an entirely different air about him. This was a bit like the old school rangering from way back in the day, a hundred years ago. He tugged down the front of his Stetson hat and nodded to Trooper Jim Conklin.

"Conklin, did you say there'd be a chopper readily available if we flush this feller out and run into a snag?" McIntyre asked. His whole countenance seemed to convey that he only tolerated other members of the party, and the fact that they were commissioned law enforcement was of little significance to him.

"We can have one here at Pine Springs within two hours from the time you boys give us a holler," Conklin replied. He seemed to be sizing up this McIntyre character who had him a place up around Weed, New Mexico. For his tracking ability, McIntyre was legend; for his people skills and moral code he was more notorious than famous.

Conklin was not alone in his reservations about Arlo McIntyre. Percy Whitmore had done a background check on this rough-and-tumble lion hunter. McIntyre wasn't unfamiliar with jail cell accommodations in several states in the Southwest, and even one or two in old Mexico. He may well have rotted away to a miserable death in old Mexico save for he was fluent in Spanish and had worked for stockmen, and sometimes even the Federales who knew him down there. McIntyre would ply his trade anywhere someone would put up the money and cover his incidental expenses. Somehow even the slickest of conniving cheapskates had little stomach for wanting to pull any fast ones on Arlo. Be that as it may, it was rumored that he'd gotten crosswise with some drug smugglers and coyotes down there about a year ago and wasn't all that anxious to cross over the Rio Grande anytime soon. Simple fact was that no matter how big or tough the man, a well-placed chunk of lead could put things in a whole different perspective.

Whitmore noted with some reservation that McIntyre had a scoped 30:06 Springfield in his rifle scabbard, and it was common knowledge he was quite efficient with the tools of his trade.

Deputy Slaughter was with the group and two other men wearing deputy uniforms, Vasquez and Amador. A park ranger named Sullivan also accompanied them as sort of a local representative of NPS jurisdiction. McIntyre paid little notice to the ranger and deferred any commentary primarily to Percy Whitmore. It seemed an eclectic collection of professionals after what many believed was at best a material witness.

The horses snorted and proceeded forward, resigned to the task ahead of them and not knowing what all it involved or for how long. The line of horses advanced at a quick walk, as the dogs had not as yet picked up a scent trail. This would change several thousand feet higher and a couple of hours later.

On a hunch, McIntyre had led the party through an area called The Bowl, a primarily coniferous forest with ridges encircling it to indeed resemble somewhat a bowl. He had proceeded eastward toward Rader Ridge and had picked up a definite scent somewhere past the Bear Canyon trail. The hounds went ballistic, baying and howling, tails wagging, noses to the ground, and traveling as quick as they could follow the scent.

Percy Whitmore felt the adrenaline rush through his system and assumed likely the same was felt by everyone else in the party. Deputy Slaughter had an almost over excited look of "let's go get 'im" on his face, and Whitmore decided right then and there that this ole boy was likely a loose cannon. There hadn't been time for a character assessment from his colleague, Trooper Jim Conklin, although he thought he noted a look of mild disgust when Conklin had looked in Slaughter's direction. People communicated a whole lot of other ways than just with the mouth Percy had learned over the years. Man, did they ever communicate...and he drifted off in reflection of Cassie Mack in spite of the excitement at hand...

"Someone call in that chopper just in case we need it!" McIntyre hollered as he muscled back on the horse's reins more than he needed to, possibly just to make it sway to and fro in confusion. McIntyre was accustomed to holding the reins, calling the shots. When he said it was time to dance you'd better dance. There was rarely anyone who dared to oppose him...

CHAPTER 23

The Good Times Are Coming

Cassie Mack had somewhat reluctantly agreed to Charlie Knox taking her to dinner and a movie—trying to get information from her. She had noticed, however, that he seemed somehow different this night. Quite frankly, he smelled better and had apparently showered and gotten a haircut. Something else seemed to be missing –perhaps it was the absence of alcohol reeking through his pores.

There was no figuring some men, and no doubt they felt the same way about women. God knows they had a right to. She dearly hoped Knox wasn't going through some mid-life crisis and trying to put the move on her. If so, he would be in for a very rude awakening. He had initially trapped her by asking if she liked Western movies, to which she applied in the affirmative.

"Well, there's a new Lee Marvin film, *Monte Walsh,* playing down at the Cinema Theater. It'd do you good to get out and engage in some innocent, frivolous fun." Charlie's offer was almost, well, almost fatherly. Charlie conscientiously smashed out his twenty-third—and final—cigarette of the day, cognizant that the habit might be an unpleasant distraction to Miss Cassie, as it was obvious she did not smoke. Besides, Charlie was quitting, well, at least cutting down.

Joe Mack had been powerfully on Cassie's mind that day, and when Mama Cass Elliot sang the theme song for the movie, *The Good Times Are Comin',* she nearly broke down in tears before the opening credits were over. Knox had noticed through his peripheral vision but seemed to be at a loss for words as to what to say. Then again, it just could be that he was more in tune than she knew.

Cassie held out some hope for Knox to be a gentleman but throughout the film was on guard for him to be somehow forward or inappropriate. She wondered who the guy was, really.

Perhaps her mind was just overwhelmed due to the events of the past year or two. Joe Mack getting home from the service—some of the bad nightmares and mood swings that he had, his desire to isolate himself. It had been hard for him over there, no doubt, but it was hard for her on the home front too. There was the affair with the rig hand from Hobbs and, of course, memories of numerous other dubious characters who only wanted to get in her pants. Now there was Joe Mack on the run amid one of the biggest manhunts since the cavalry pursued Chief Victorio in this part of the country. And here she was now; in a movie theater with a private detective whose loyalties she was still trying to figure out.

"Can I get you some popcorn, young lady?" Charlie leaned toward her with a wholesome earnest smile, as if he knew something wonderful and couldn't wait to share it with her.

"Sure, why not? Thank you."

"How about something to drink?"

"Dr. Pepper if they have it."

"Why shore they do—that's what I drink whenever I come here! I'll be right back hon, okay? Can I get you anything else?"

"No, no, thank you, you've done plenty already."

Cassie plunged herself back into the film and was enthralled by the scene where it appeared that Lee Marvin would be willing to marry the leading lady. As the film reel turned, however, it was apparent that he would not be willing to do anything that would jeopardize his being a cowboy—including committing to someone. Cassie didn't know if it was hormones or what, but the tears started to flow from her eyes, down her cheeks, making ever so subtle furrows in her makeup that would never be revealed in the dark anyway.

"Here you go, young lady!" Charlie whispered loudly with that brand new beaming smile.

"Thank you, Charlie, that was nice of you."

"Miss Cassie—ma'am—are you alright?"

"What do you mean?"

"Well, uh, er, it looks like you've been crying."

"Oh, it's just the movie, that's all. There was kind of a sad scene while you were out getting popcorn. I'm all right, really."

They sat there silent for the remainder of the film munching on popcorn and sipping on the ice-cold sodas. The theater had a modest crowd this evening, perhaps because it was a week night, and perhaps because a lot of people didn't spare money for such frivolity.

They walked out while the theme song played once again and exited into the warm night air in Roswell. To her surprise, Charlie got the car door for her—just like she was a real lady—and closed it gently behind her. She could tell it was contrary to his previous self and, frankly, she wondered what the hell was going on.

"Miss Cassie," Charlie began before he turned the key in the ignition, "I've got something at the office I think you might like to see—would you mind?" he asked with that still full of newness, wholesome smile.

"Gosh, I don't know, Charlie, it's getting late, and I've got to work the morning shift tomorrow..."

"It won't take but a couple of minutes, honest. I feel like there's something special I'm really supposed to share with you."

Oh, great, here it comes, she thought, this ole boy's going to try to put the hustle on me. I'm so tired of being treated like a piece of breeding stock...

"It's really quite late, Mr. Knox, I should go home..."

"Please don't get mad at me, but I followed you to that little Baptist church the other day," he blurted out.

That caught her off guard. Where was this guy coming from, and what did he know that was such almighty good news?

"Followed me—why?" she asked a little irritated.

"I have to outright admit that I initially hoped you were having a rendezvous with your husband Joe. Miss Cassie, I have only the most honorable intentions in this case. I believe your story, I believe your eyes. I want to clear your husband and see you kids get back together again; it's too late for me, but I really, really want..."

At this point, the crusty private eye turned his head to the side in a futile attempt to hide the tears that were welling up in his eyes.

"Mr. Knox, I have to say, you are acting very out of character tonight. What is going on? You're not—I'm sorry—*drunk*—are you?"

Still looking away, Knox raised up his hand nearest to her in defiance, then slowly turned his head and said, "Oh, no, I'm not drunk. That's just it—I'm stone sober for once—and at this hour of the night. Please don't think me crazy, Miss Cassie, but you're sort of becoming the daughter I never had. I haven't done much noble in my life for anyone, and I'd really like to do so now. I'm convinced your husband is innocent and I want to help prove it and get you two back together again—where you belong. I wish I'd had someone giving me some mentoring years ago when I was married..." He trailed off with his eyes getting glassy again.

By now he had started the car and *I'll Never Find Another You* by the Seekers was playing on the radio. Judith Durham's beautiful voice mesmerized them and both sat in silence wondering what in the world was going on this evening.

"Go ahead, Charlie, it's all right."

"Ma'am?"

"Show me whatever it is you were going to show me at your office—as long as it won't take too long."

"No, ma'am, not to worry, it won't take long at all." Charlie reassured her. They drove on in silence the ten minutes to his office/apartment building. The song continued to play on the radio with a voice that tore at her heart; for a moment, in her fantasies, she was the lead vocalist, this was her message to Joe Mack, "*If I should lose your love dear I don't know what I'd do, for I know I'd never find another you...*'"

When the song ended, Charlie shut the radio off. He cast a glance at her then commented ever so understandingly, "It's an awfully touching song, isn't it?"

Cassie was the one looking out her window now, as once again this evening tears flowed down her cheeks. She merely nodded her head in the affirmative as it was too hard to answer with words right then.

Charlie Knox is a man who stands five feet eleven inches tall, weighs 215 pounds. He likes taking walks through the park on a fall day, shuffling his feet through the dry, fallen leaves. In his mind, he knows he has an appointment with destiny, that he is on the downward slope of the rollercoaster and that things are moving faster and faster. He knows that once it hits bottom then shoots skyward, his eyes will never leave the sky again. To Charlie, it is not insanity, it is a vision.

Charlie eased the car to a stop outside his building, then got out and opened the door for Cassie. They went inside and he clomped up the weathered old wooden stair treads. Not everything about him had changed at least. He made distinct clomping sounds when he walked; he had a certain trademark swagger that could make you believe he was apathetical about life, or lazy. She followed him up the stairs and stood to the side of the dim light while he fumbled with his keys in the lock. He opened the heavily varnished door with its frosted glass window and his name painted on it, "Charles Knox Private Investigative Services." He flipped on the dim light in the office and a desk lamp before before motioning for her to take a seat.

"Have a seat, Miss Cassie, please."

She accepted his offer and sat down in the old oak chair, feeling somewhat unnerved with the evening so far and, ironically, emotionally drained. She hoped this would be brief so she could get home and sort out her thoughts. Perhaps Joe Mack had tried to call while she was gone. Perhaps there was something about him on the TV news.

"Miss Cassie, I've gotten some recent revelation about how we need to go about bringing this to a proper resolve against all odds. There's an awful lot of legal heat building up and, darlin', to be honest with you it don't look all that good. I know I'm not the most polished man you ever come across—definitely not refined in social graces. I fully realize that I'm a day late and a dollar short in most things in life, but something really came to me while I was visiting with that preacher acquaintance of yours—Pastor Jack Shafer." Charlie pulled a stiff-paged, brand new Bible out of his desk drawer, but in numerous places scraps of paper had been stuck in to mark key passages.

Smiling like a cat that just caught a bird, he opened up the Bible and started to share with Cassie...

CHAPTER 24

Fox On The Run

Joe Mack had long cleared McKittrick Canyon and was actually following the Bell Springs drainage to Highway 62-180 when he encountered the wetbacks in their temporary camp. There were four of them, a couple perhaps in their forties, a teenaged daughter, and a boy of perhaps ten years of age.

"Buenos tardes!" he greeted them with what little Spanish he knew.

"Buenos tardes," the father figure replied looking a bit apprehensive.

"Como se llama?" He asked their names as a polite, reassuring gesture.

There was Alberto, Olivia, young Miguel, and Belinda. It was Belinda, the pretty teenaged girl who spoke fluent English. It was apparent the whole family had some level of understanding of his words, though they were not as proficient as Belinda.

Joe Mack told them there was no need to worry, that he himself was on the run from the law for a crime which he only discovered and had not committed. He gambled and even told them the full story, and who he suspected, Salvador Quionnes, the wool buyer.

When he said the name, the girl looked in shock at her mother and father and they spoke rapidly and excitedly in Spanish. Every now and then one is reminded what a small world it can be, even in this vast expanse of Chihuahuan Desert which lapped over the border of two countries.

"We know of this, Salvador," Belinda began, "He has a very evil reputation, and it is rumored that he has raped and murdered many girls down in Mexico as well as up here in the United States of America. He is called," then she asked her father something in Spanish and he thought a moment and replied, "Shrike." "He is called alcaudon the butcher bird or shrike." She looked around at the shrubbery and finally spied what she was looking for. "Look here, señor, here is what the shrike does," she exclaimed, pointing. There, impaled on the sharp end of a broken tiny branch, was a horned lizard. The lizard had been impaled through the eyeball and left to die on the branch for a meal later on. Its macabre, mummified body was a testimony to its predator's barbarous tactics.

Belinda continued on after a pause about Quionnes, "He has been questioned by the police from time to time, but he and his brother have lots of money and he bribes them not to pursue any leads."

Joe Mack was shocked to the point that he had to find a smooth boulder to sit down on and clear his head. The recognition had been instant. Somehow, this was the lead he needed. Young Belinda was incomprehensibly beautiful with her black hair, dark brown eyes, and gentle face. Her eyes were like the beautiful eyes of a doe. Joe Mack figured her to be sixteen or seventeen, although one could never be sure. She had a peaceful countenance about her which he felt drawn to. Quickly he chastised himself inside for wishing he were seven or eight years younger. He was, he argued in his mind, a reasonably young man after all. It was natural to be attracted to one so beautiful and, he discerned, kind and loving. But then again, he was married—technically—and he must not lose hope or focus of restoring his relationship with Cassie, mending old wounds, and moving forward to better days ahead.

"My friends," he began, "I have to run now—I have to prove my innocence and this Salvador's guilt—somehow. I don't ask that you allow yourselves to get caught by the posse that is surely following me, but if you do, please tell them the story about this monster who has terrorized both sides of the Rio Grande."

With that he shook hands with the father and took off from their camp spiraling around it a couple of times to confuse any dogs which might be on his trail. He zigzagged through mazes of prickly pear cactus and a dense patch of lechuguilla. The lechuguilla were like knife blades growing through the ground and could go through a man's boot and cripple him, much less a dog.

Joe Mack noticed a semi-tanker truck parked along the highway ahead. Perhaps the driver was taking a nap or relieving himself. Joe Mack didn't know. However, he made for the highway as quickly as he could. This truck was headed north toward Carlsbad, New Mexico. His heart started pounding more from excitement at first, then from exertion as he realized the severity of his situation. The truck was a fuel tanker from Mexico; good chance the driver would be oblivious to the no doubt highly publicized manhunt that Joe was the target of.

He looked behind him and could barely hear the all too familiar sounds of a helicopter in the distance. It appeared to be flying over the McKittrick Canyon drainage and to the high country to the west of there. There was no time to lose; that bird could be flying the countryside for no one but him.

Brazenly, Joe Mack approached the driver who had been taking a lunch break along the highway in the driver's seat.

"Que paso!" he greeted the driver, then gestured with his thumb and asked, "Carlsbad?"

"Si, señor, Carlsbad, Hobbs, Seminole," the driver replied in broken English. He was affably letting Joe know that he was going even further than Carlsbad should need be.

"Muchas gracias, mi amigo, muchas gracias!" Joe exclaimed as he got into the truck cab on the passenger side.

Mexican music was playing on the radio, and a cup of coffee steamed from a thermos cup in a console holder. The driver was finishing a burrito, and Joe Mack must have looked on with obvious interest.

"You like cafe, hombre, burrito? Uh, es mucho carne. I have plenty, amigo."

Even the broken English was a blessing, and Joe Mack accepted the man's generosity. He ate and drank ravenously, and the driver pointed out a bottle of water on the floorboard. The water was tepid, unlike the crisp cool water of Bell Springs, but it slaked his thirst and he was getting a glimmer of hope.

Soon they crossed the state line from Texas into New Mexico, going through the Gypsum Hills on through White City and the entrance to Carlsbad Caverns National Park. They were near the small airport outside the town of Carlsbad when Joe Mack pondered packing a rifle once he was let out in town. Better to lose it right now, he thought.

"Señor—you take my rifle?" he queried with a smile.

The driver looked at it and pointed to himself questioningly.

"Si, señor—you take rifle—me amigo!"

The driver excitedly agreed and shook his hand. Besides, there would be no rifle to confiscate and test ballistics on if he were caught. In forty-eight hours, it would be banished forever south of the border to be used on mule deer and mountain lions by some other owner.

He had the driver let him off just outside of town, where he slipped into a large culvert under the highway and changed from his tattered camouflage fatigues into blue jeans and a civilian shirt. He cleaned up a little with a bottle of water the driver had given him, combed his hair, and tried to look more civilized so as not to stand out when he got into town.

Joe Mack went into a thrift shop and purchased a large straw cowboy hat, used but nice, some sunglasses, and an old guitar. There would be less suspicion of a cowboy walking around with a guitar. A man on the run doesn't usually bring along a bulky musical instrument for company.

He got to a pay phone and dialed Cassie. It rang. It rang and rang some more.

Not home obviously, perhaps at work, getting groceries or whatever. The frustration level was high, but he would simply have to keep trying. In the meantime, he would have to keep a low profile and not draw the attention of the local police.

An urban environment has unique challenges. On one hand, he could blend in with the scattered crowds; on the other, it seemed as though he had no single refuge to just hole up in and rest a good while. He had a friend or two in town, but considered it risky to contact them, and he didn't want to jeopardize their safety in the process.

Wary of staying in any one place too long, Joe walked into a grocery store. He freshened up in the bathroom as best he could and marveled at how nice the air conditioning felt. He grabbed a cart and started walking around in no apparent hurry.

When he went down the aisle with the personal hygiene products, he stopped short with his mouth agape as he stared at the beautiful blonde-haired woman who had been his wife for several years.

She was not facing him, but he recognized her features nonetheless. Cassie was intently shopping and reading a label or price tag. Joe looked up at a shelf and picked up some disposable razors and a can of shaving cream. Suddenly an idea hit him and he eased up behind Cassie and spoke to her in a soft, casual voice.

"Cassie, don't look up, but come meet me in the greeting card section," and he moved on down the aisle.

Cassie whipped her head around in astonishment, wide eyed and her heart pounding. It was so unexpected, it was like a dream. She forced herself to regain her composure and nonchalantly continued looking at some items, then proceeded over to the next aisle where the greeting cards were. Oh, how she had wanted to shout for joy and run and hug Joe—if indeed a hug from her would be welcome. Better instincts prevailed, and she thanked God that she hadn't over reacted.

There he was—Joe Mack—fugitive from justice. Cowboy. Marine. Viet Nam veteran. Estranged husband and friend. Friend—what a sacred title, she thought.

As if it were the poker game of the century, they pretended masterfully not to know each other and to read through the special birthday cards and thinking-of-you cards.

Pounding hearts, sweaty palms, and spikes in adrenaline attempted to undermine what they projected through behavior on the exterior.

"Excuse me, sir," Cassie said as she reached a bit in front of Joe to select a card to look at. She wasn't looking at him directly, though she desperately wanted to.

"Oh, certainly," Joe replied shifting his body position a little. How he wanted to grab hold of her and kiss her and hug her—right here in the grocery store! But, he knew he couldn't.

"Hmmmm," she muttered while looking at a card, then ever so subtly looking around to see if there was anyone nearby. There was not.

"What do we do?" she asked.

"La Caverna Hotel. Get us a room as soon as you leave here. Make sure you're not followed, even if you have to leave your car here. We'll talk there."

Now Joe Mack reached for a card, excusing himself. He appeared to be intently studying it, and spoke ever so softly, "I love you, Cassie. See you in a while."

Cassie Mack didn't reply, but finished her shopping and checked out of the store.

She disobeyed Joe's advice about the car, parked it a short distance away, and carefully exited her car and walked the little extra distance to the La Caverna Hotel.

It was weird and exciting somehow—for crying out loud—she felt as though she were about to have an affair with someone at a motel—only this someone was technically and legally—her husband.

"May I help you ma'am?" the desk clerk asked.

Fortunately, Cassie did not know the gentleman and vice versa. But then, she was from Roswell, not Carlsbad, and didn't truly know that many people here.

"I'd like a room for the night, please."

"Are you alone?"

"Yes. Well, no actually, my husband will be joining me shortly. He's, he should be here soon."

Her pulse was starting to quicken for reasons she wasn't even sure of. Fear of law enforcement catching Joe before she held him was certainly one concern.

"Will a queen-sized single bed suffice then?" the man inquired.

"Yes, that will be fine," she replied, wondering if he believed her story or assumed her to be some cheap slut or adulteress out for a good time with her boyfriend. God knows she had been down that road and was worried that even a complete stranger could see the sins on her soul as though she were transparent.

She paid the man, then sat down in the lobby reading a magazine until Joe Mack finally showed up.

They tried desperately to appear almost indifferent to one another. As though there really wasn't any burning desire on either's behalf. And yet, the opposite was true.

Cassie stuck the key in the lock and started to open the door when Joe surprised her by picking her up and carrying her across the threshold.

"What do you think about that, Mrs. Mack?" He inquired with his shining blue eyes and pearly smile as he studied her approvingly.

"Oh, I approve, all right," she replied, thankful that he had such audacity, spontaneity, and flirtatiousness—even after all that had transpired in their relationship.

They set down their bags from the grocery, and in Joe's case—everything he owned for the moment.

"Oh, Cassie!" he gasped, and grasped her tightly to his chest, kissing her passionately and long on her lips. She smelled wonderful, felt wonderful in his arms at last.

"Oh, Joe, I'm so sorry, I, I—please forgive me."

"Of course, I forgive you—you know me. It will take some time though—to sort things out and all. But I don't ever want you to leave me again. I definitely have my faults; I'm not squeaky clean in my life either, you know."

Their passion for one another burned perhaps more than it ever had before in the lifetime that they had known each other. They sat down on the bed, embracing and kissing each other.

For both it was a burning passionate episode they had longed for and had feared might never happen again. Then again, it could be near the end of everything. They entangled themselves much as they did on their honeymoon some years prior, lost in everything else but comfort, love, and desire for each other. In some ways, it seemed like a dream that was too good to believe; in a way, there was an even more special something between them now, welded by the white hot fire of forgiveness. It was as though—suddenly there was a gentle knock on the door of their room!

Cassie and Joe sat up with the sheets clutched to their naked bodies staring in horror at the door. Who could it be? Was it the law? Was it motel management? Someone else. Suddenly a familiar voice summoned Cassie from the other side, a voice that she knew, but Joe did not!

CHAPTER 25

A Matter of Trust

"Miss Cassie, are you in there?" came the voice. It was Knox! Cassie's heart started pounding wildly in her chest, and Joe felt as though his heart was in his throat.

"Who is that?" he queried in a stifled, somewhat hoarse whisper.

"The private investigator I was telling you about! Knox!"

"He must have spotted you and followed you here. Didn't you leave the car at the grocery store?"

There was no need for a reply, and Knox once again knocked on the door, a little louder this time, with the same inquiry. He had recently put out his twelfth and final cigarette of the day. He was making some progress in the health department and silently, in his mind, he congratulated himself. It became obvious to Joe and Cassie that they would have to take their chances and meet with the man, poor timing though it was.

"Yes, Mr. Knox, just wait a minute," Cassie replied nervously.

Joe looked out the window and considered his options for escape, and Cassie observed his stare. She was reading his mail, his very thoughts.

"It's got to end, doesn't it?" Joe asked.

Cassie merely answered with those compassionate blue eyes, which were starting to tear up as she hastily dressed while Joe did the same. She straightened her hair in the bathroom mirror, and Joe straightened up the bedding. In a way, Joe Mack was somewhat relieved; perhaps things would somehow end up better than him getting shot like a rabid dog without so much as getting to tell his version of what happened near Salt Flat.

Resignedly, Cassie accepted the fact that her hair was less than perfect and that she looked a bit "tousled." Frankly, she didn't give a damn at this point. If this crusty, recently born-again Christian private eye assumed that she had had a good romp in the bedroom with her estranged husband—so be it—she was proud of it. She reached for the door handle and opened it.

Charlie Knox stood there for a moment with his hat in his hand and a slight hint of a blush on his face. He was doing his utmost best to be tactful and sensitive given the obvious situation, but at best it was an awkward moment.

"You know, I'm actually pretty beside myself with joy at what I perceive has happened this day," Knox began, "I know I'm not the sharpest tack in the box, but it looks to me as if here is one marriage that's not going to settle for going down in flames. You kids aren't like many of those free love, dope smokin' hippies runnin' around the country with a devil-may-care attitude."

The comments were certainly received well by Joe Mack, and Cassie as well. Joe liked this rough around the edges investigator and his frank candor.

Knox fidgeted with his hat, unable to pace about in the small motel room. He looked about at a couple of chairs, then back at Joe and Cassie, "May I?" he asked.

"Sure, sure," Joe replied. He and Cassie sat on the edge of the bed, looking toward Charlie Knox in anticipation of some sort of fatherly advice, some master plan to deliver them from the nightmare that had become their life.

Charlie Knox had a pensive expression while he rubbed his chin with his massive right hand—as if that physical ritual was going to conjure up some kind of powerful revelation or profound direction. It was obvious his mind was tortured and he hesitated, not wanting to rush in and scare off these two fugitives.

"You know, it's not as though you two are Bonnie and Clyde or something. You know, Bonnie and Clyde did stop in Carlsbad to hide out a bit at a relative's place while they were on the run—it's true. Fact is they kidnapped Deputy Sheriff Joe Johns at Bonnie's aunt's farm near Carlsbad. That was before y'all's time; heck, I wasn't but a child myself back then. But you kids aren't like those two murdering bank robbers. You didn't hurt anybody, did you, Joe?"

"No. I assume Cassie told you my side of the story already."

"Yes, as a matter a fact she did indeed. She also told me you had a suspect of your own—want to tell me about that?"

"Quionnes Wool Buyers. I believe the Mescin feller from that Quionnes outfit might well be our man. Furthermore, I came across some wetbacks in the Guadalupes who were familiar with that serpent and claimed that he's been terrorizing young women and families on both sides of the Rio Grande for some time."

Knox dutifully penned some notes in a small black notebook while Joe Mack divulged what he knew. It was true, Charlie Knox maybe wasn't the sharpest tack in the box, but he had a work ethic, and he had drive, and principles.

"Uh hum, uh hum," Knox muttered as he jotted down notes while Joe Mack rambled on in that West Texas drawl.

Finally, at length, Knox closed his eyes after absorbing everything he had written down. He sucked in a deep breath then exhaled and shrugged his shoulders.

"I have a plan," he began, "and at this point it's purely a matter of trust on y'all's behalf. You can trust me to do what's best for you or not. It's up to your discernment whether or not you consider me a trustworthy man..."

From there a masterful plan was hatched in the La Caverna hotel room with three people thrown together by fate—or by God? Knox disclosed his plan to bait and trap this Salvador Quionnes—and everyone present would be involved. He had done his homework, and certainly Joe Mack had just given him some more valuable intel. Knox knew people south of the border as well—people who owed him, believe it or not. He would set a trap for this West Texas predator and lure him into it with a victim. That victim would be none other than Cassie Mack!

"Are you crazy, mister?" Joe Mack demanded, reflexively angry at the thought of jeopardizing his wife on such a scheme, putting his trust in some crusty old investigator he had never laid eyes on before in his life.

"You got a better idea, Joe? You're a hunted man. I could be in trouble right now for not turning you over to the proper authorities. In a way, I've done my part—I found you. But at this point, I'm working more on Miss Cassie's behalf, although the Texas Rangers might have a different viewpoint, particularly Percival Pinkerton Whitmore."

Percy Whitmore. Joe Mack thought for a moment that he caught a troubled look or almost guilt on Cassie's face at the sound of this man's name. Again, Whitmore was someone else Joe Mack had never spoken to. He wouldn't know him if he brushed shoulders with him on the street. That was unfortunate because no doubt Whitmore would know him. Joe had to inquire of Cassie about this Ranger Whitmore. He knew she had talked with him.

"What about this Ranger—Percival Whitmore, Cassie? What's your take on him?

Do you trust him?"

Cassie looked back at Joe with eyes that seemed to have an unexplained nervousness. For a while, there was just an uncomfortable silence...

CHAPTER 26

Percival Pinkerton Whitmore

Percy looked over the case files on his cluttered desk in his El Paso office, still fuming over the missed opportunity to corral Joe Mack into custody in the Guadalupes. He had given them the slip, and that was a feat not easily done to the likes of Arlo McIntyre. McIntyre had fairly well thrown a fit once it was discovered Joe Mack

must have made it to the highway and hitchhiked a ride to God knows where—east, west, north, or south. Percy's assumption was north to Carlsbad or Roswell. Already a net was being cast in that whole region with a variety of law enforcement entities.

Percy took a sip of tepid coffee and frowned at it as he gulped it down. He felt at his shirt pocket to reassure himself that the Cuban cigars were still there. Yes. Later perhaps. Percy buried his face in his hands for a moment and massaged his weary face muscles as his elbows rested on his oak desk. He pushed back his hair in a fatigued effort to appear forever well groomed, then gazed out the second-story window of his office. East. He was looking east in the general direction of the Guadalupes, and Carlsbad, New Mexico, and Van Horn, Texas.

Suddenly, a pale-faced Mary Clark appeared in his office door with a troubled look on her beautiful, middle-aged face.

"Mr. Whitmore," she began, "it's Helen. She's tried to kill herself and is being admitted to the El Paso Community Hospital as we speak..."

"What? What happened, how do you know?"

"Your neighbor called the ambulance; he heard a commotion and discovered she had jumped into the pool, uh, very intoxicated."

"Is she—is she okay?"

"They think your neighbor saved her life, but you'd better get over to the hospital right away. Mr. Percy if there is anything I can do?" she offered with worry etched deeply in her brow.

"No, Mary, thank you. I appreciate it, but I don't know what that could be."

Percy threw on his sport coat and grabbed his Stetson off the hat rack as he headed out the door of his office. He had been down this road before, but it was never pleasant, and to some extent he always assumed a certain level of responsibility for her welfare. The timing was terrible, of course. He still cared for Helen, but he didn't know how to break the yoke of burden that the alcohol had put on her life. He had battled the same issue some years ago, but broke clean of it. Then again, he wasn't the one driving the car under the influence years ago when their son died in that tragic crash...

Percival Pinkerton Whitmore is a man. Stands 5'11" tall, wears starched and ironed Wrangler jeans, white Western-cut shirts and a white Stetson hat. He relishes a cold glass of unsweetened iced tea with a slice of lemon, roasted long green chilies in season, and barbeque brisket at any time. He is a traditionalist, conservative in his values. He has that "salt and pepper" look in his well-groomed, short hair and close cropped mustache. He prides himself on being a Christian man, though he rarely darkens the door of a church or makes liberal expression of his faith. His time in the Marines and with the Rangers is time permanently branded in his memory, in his character, in his being.

He is a man who, for the moment, has no dreams for the future, as he fears his future will find him totally alone. He dwells at times in the past, sometimes dreads the present, but buries himself in the task at hand. Work. The mission, the case, the assignment. His work is paramount to his existence. Without his work, he questions whether he will have any value or worth. Although a Christian man, he questions his own salvation—even though he was weaned on the doctrine of once saved, always saved. No, Percy must work out his salvation with fear and trembling. Other people's perception of him is important to him, although he doesn't let it dictate his every move.

Percy notes that the palms of his hands are sweaty and his heart is pounding rapidly as he speeds toward the hospital. Mary has thought to call the local police, who provide a speedy escort as he races to the hospital. One of these attempts might well be Helen's last; possibly, this could be the last. Where did their love go? What could he possibly do to assuage her anguish—their anguish—over the irreversible loss of their son? Was he unforgiving and she knew it? Was there anything he could do to minister to her? Perhaps think to pray for her or attend church once in a while? Yet, he had tried all these things, apparently to no avail. He must persevere—he must—for her sake, and his as well.

His mind drifted back to those many years ago when they first met. He had been drawn to her good looks, initially, but her adventurous spirit and contagious humor hooked him for keeps. She had been fun in those days, and her inhibitions were never noticeable and even less so after a drink or three. At the time, he dismissed it as nothing more than the recklessness of youth, never imagining that she had acquired a taste for something that would demolish heaven on earth.

Helen's parents had been prominent El Pasoans. They had envisioned Helen marrying an oil tycoon or even someone of prominence with the railroad, a building contractor, manufacturer, or real estate broker. In this regard, Percy had been a disappointment. To them, he was nothing more than a simple West Texas cowboy with a badge, and perhaps a bit of a reputation. They conceded that much at least. They'd had a penchant for the fine things in life, in society, parties, and booze. While Helen's father had an affinity for fine Scotch, her mother liked her martinis. Tragically, they both perished on a yacht in a storm off the coast of Belize some twenty years prior and had never even seen their only grandson pitch an inning of baseball.

Granted, there was an inheritance. It explained why Percy lived in a nicer home on sizable acreage that was nicer than what his boss or his boss's boss lived in. Yet, funny how money can't necessarily buy happiness. Percy was convinced he knew people who lived with not half as much but were twice as happy. His home had a swimming pool and a nice little pecan grove. Back in the day, Helen could make a heavenly pecan pie—when she was sober enough and had the mind to.

Percy eased off the accelerator as he approached the entrance to the hospital. He had so much work to do, yet this was important. He didn't want to lose Helen. He despised what she had become, yet he comprehended it somewhat as well. Part of him agonized over whether he was partly to blame for the mental state she was in. How he longed for better days—more sober days when he was regarded as the suave, devilishly handsome cowboy that Helen had been so smitten with and, conversely, she had been in Percy's eyes the beautiful El Paso debutante, a girl of beauty and affluence beyond his wildest dreams. He missed the simple things: picnics, horseback rides, long drives with no agenda and no destination out in the desert. Lying on a slab of limestone somewhere on a moonlit night staring up at the magnificent display of stars in the sky and sharing lighthearted, romantic conversations. Then, for just a sinful moment, he drifted off wondering if he would have been better off with a simple, more dependent type like Cassie Mack. My but she was lovely, and attractive in ways he dare not ponder. He pushed through the glass entrance doors to the hospital, trying to shift his thoughts to a more loyal and noble focus, to cease his adulterous fantasies...

CHAPTER 27

Charlie's Quest

Knox had hidden the fugitive and his estranged bride in his own apartment. Far beyond that, he had hired a cleaning woman to clean his room, the bathroom and his place in general to make it more desirable and presentable to this young couple. He gave them every courtesy, every nicety that he could afford or imagine. It was imperative to him that they remain in the safety of his home where he could safeguard them until the trap was sprung and the real rat in this entire, onerous affair was killed.

Despite his recent born-again conversion, Charlie couldn't help but feel a little smug about the connections he had south of the border. Reyes had given him plenty of information, well worth the price of Charlie buying him lunch in the little café over the river in Santa Elena in Big Bend country. Sure, he had given him a little money as well, but Charlie and Reyes were old amigos from way back. It was in that tiny village of Santa Elena that Charlie learned of the insidious predator who had attacked many a young maiden on both sides of the border, only to elude capture due to bribes and payoffs from Quionnes and his partner brother. The vermin did not come from a prosperous family, but they had come into affluence somehow, whether through legitimate shrewd dealing in the wool trade or otherwise. The rape/murder victims were, of course, robbed as well, but typically didn't have much of monetary value on them. Many had been hitchhikers and were living on scant means.

Charlie Knox had his past, his regrets. Were he to tell anyone, they would claim him crazy or suicidal, but somehow he knew that his time on this mortal earth was short. Funny, but he was good with that. He was actually somewhat relieved and even anticipated the opportunity to dwell with his Lord and savior, Jesus Christ! He—Charlie Knox! Imagine that! A nobody come somebody special at the last moment!

Almost jubilantly, Knox whistled a tune, the theme from *Monte Walsh*, and in a soft tone sang some of the lyrics, "*...the good times are coming, they're coming real soon, and I'm not just pitchin' pennies at the moon...*"

Knox *was* Monte Walsh, in a way. He was set in his ways and unable or unwilling to learn any other means of making a living this late in his life. The love of his life was dead by now, no doubt, and he could never attract another this late in the game, who could replace her? Vicariously, he lived through the lives of others, and in the most earnest way he wanted something exceedingly beautiful to come about in the lives of Joe and Cassie Mack. He wanted those two kids to have a life more beautiful than one could imagine. He wanted them to somehow remember the good intentions of a simple private investigator by the name of Charlie Knox as they lived out their lives. It was truly beautiful to be so obsessed with blessing the lives of someone other than himself.

Knox totally understood Joe's apprehension at using Cassie for live bait to lure in one of the most insidious monsters to prey in the desert southwest in recent memory. But through visiting and sharing issues of the heart they came to realize that, in a way, they were now an inseparable trio, that everything hinged on teamwork and success.

Oh, yes, Knox had done his homework all right, maybe better than the Texas Rangers had or other law enforcement entities. He knew the routine routes and schedules that vermin Quionnes had been taking. To merely apprehend the rat would, of course, result in him lying, and no physical evidence to hold him. It was a cinch he wouldn't just come clean and confess his heinous crimes. That sort likely wouldn't do so with their dying breath save for wanting the glory in a sick way for their actions. No, that's why he would have Cassie wait alongside the road with a disabled vehicle just prior to his arrival. She would wear a head band and some "hippie" attire to look like a free spirit. Knox pulled no punches and was certain his trap would be a success. No detail was too small to lure in this stinking skunk. She would go shopping tomorrow for hippie clothes, maybe even some Janis Joplin-type sunglasses and a peace sign necklace. She was told to go bra-less and to wear tight-fitting, hip-hugging bell bottom jeans. If they could find a used, worn pair, so much the better. If need be, they would offer a ridiculous price to some girl on the street of comparable size.

Charlie Knox felt a certain level of comfort and security having Joe and Cassie asleep in his apartment. He had contemplated putting something in the way of the front door to make noise should they get cold feet and try to flee in the night, but reconsidered. They knew as well as he knew that his plan was the only plan. Catch the real killer, the real monster, and a lot could be overlooked in the original and subsequent charges against Joe Mack. Charlie was asleep on the couch in his living room, happy as a clam that the

couple was safe in his home. At the last moment, he would notify Percy Whitmore, the Texas Ranger, about his plan. He would not allow Whitmore time to change their plans, only to arrive should the need arise and help net the scumbag should something go south.

The trap would be set up around Crow Flats, out in the middle of nowhere, and with enough people tipped off to where Quionnes would have very few choices of road to travel in this remote section of West Texas/Southeast New Mexico. Ideally he needed to be apprehended alive. Wounded would be okay, just not mortally so. Prison was where that snake needed to go, just long enough for the death penalty to be executed.

Knox had blown much of his savings even to the point of buying a used van complete with a psychedelic paint job and peace signs painted on it. It was rusty and battered, perfect for the deception. He had considered using Cassie's car but wanted something more enticing. Perhaps he could get a reimbursement from Whitmore for his incidental expenditures later on. No doubt Whitmore wouldn't appreciate being brought up to speed so late in the game; he had his own ego and agendas no doubt. Knox had noted a quirky uneasiness in Whitmore the last time he visited with him; call it crazy, but he suspected the aging Ranger had been smitten with Cassie Mack. Charlie chastised himself in his own mind; after all, hadn't he referred to her as a good looking little filly before his salvation? Aw, the things simple words can do sometimes.

Charlie glanced at his alarm clock and noted that it was about 2:30 a.m. He had best get some sleep so they could get their shopping done later today and finalize their plans for Wednesday, the day Quionnes would make his buying route through Dell City and the surrounding area en route to Weed, New Mexico. It was such a weird thing; Charlie had not felt so smug, so content—so happy—in many years. He was now down to seven cigarettes a day. He would sleep well for several hours without a care in the world. Somehow, he knew this would be his last big case before he moved on to bigger and better things. Somehow, what happened after this soon to be triumphant victory was of little concern to him.

CHAPTER 28

THE HEAD OF THE MONSTER

Salvador Quionnes drove along the West Texas back roads in a good mood this day. He had made some good deals on his wool-buying trek and had a trailer in tow behind his pickup with product that he would turn for a good profit. The Guadalupe Mountains loomed on the horizon to the east—a most majestic site he always appreciated.

He chuckled to himself a little as he heard a news clip on the radio about the fugitive from justice, Joe Mack, and the latest intelligence, which was almost nothing. In fact, he broke out laughing at the thought of the hapless gringo taking the fall for something he, Salvador Quionnes, had done! More likely than not the desperate cowboy would be killed in a volley of lead at the hands of clueless law enforcement officials wanting to appease the public with the punishment of someone for the crime committed. It would buy him some time to keep up a good image with current and prospective sellers in this region of the country. Perhaps someday when he had enough money saved up he would retire south of the border where his hard-earned U.S. dollars would go much further by Mexican standards.

Salvador liked the remoteness of this country far better than the hustle and bustle of places like El Paso and Juarez. Granted, a snake like himself could lose himself in a whole den of serpents in the city, but he preferred the life of a loner. Free to make his own decisions and take his own actions as he pleased, without an audience. His mind wandered this day in fantasies about the numerous attractive young women he had picked up and defiled, murdered, and buried. He entertained sick thoughts about what depravities he might inflict on his next victim. Perhaps a little more pain infliction, perhaps allow the next woman to plead relentlessly for mercy and longer before he dispatched her. The thought of such things aroused him sexually until he could hardly stand it.

He pulled off to the side of the road to urinate and pour himself another cup of coffee and have a cigarette. There was no rush; there was never any rush with him. He sat up on the hood of the truck and lit up a cigarette and was enjoying the placid fall day.

The desert, after all, was full of predators like himself. On little breaks such as this he observed a lot about predators and prey. Red-tailed hawks dive-bombing a prairie dog or some other rodent. Road-runners catching lizards, or perhaps a collared lizard catching a smaller whip-tailed lizard and swallowing it whole. On this occasion he observed a tarantula hawk paralyze a tarantula and drag it off to a hole somewhere. The tarantulas were actually alive when the giant wasp laid their eggs on it which would hatch out and feed on the living victim. It was Salvador's favorite predator observation. Sometimes he wished he could be that tarantula hawk; he could never get enough of inflicting pain and agony on someone, preferably someone sexual and beautiful. Out here he was the biggest predator, he was the king monster!

Aw, the memories he had, the filthy dirty secrets he had that no one totally knew. Of course, his brother knew some things; he had had to bail him out of jail a time or two, bribes some cops, or secure a crooked lawyer.

Salvador inhaled deeply on his cigarette then exhaled slowly. It was such a good day. He was at total peace. Perhaps he would have just one more cup of coffee before he resumed his buying trip.

"So many suckers!" He thought of the numerous farmers and ranchers he did business with. Some even invited him in for lunch or supper thinking he was such a nice guy. He never failed at such times to be remarkably charismatic and phony. He would mesmerize them with excessive manners, humorous wit, and flattery. Meanwhile, in his filthy, depraved mind he would fantasize about their wives and daughters while breaking bread with them. A time or two, when the circumstances were right, he even asked the blessing before they ate a meal. It was outrageously amusing to him. There were absolutely no limits to his hypocrisy or audacity!

At last he decided he must proceed onward if he was to get home before dark, and he had several more stops to make. Seldom did he see any vehicles out on this stretch as he was getting farther away from the irrigated cropland and out into the harsh desert, which he preferred. Less people here, far less people. He hadn't attained his speed for very long when he noted a vehicle up ahead stopped alongside the road. It wasn't just any vehicle, but a van, and its hood was up. Salvador slowed down as this section of the road had a bit of a wind to it, and he didn't want by happenchance to collide with someone else passing this vehicle. There were some harsh rugged little mountains to the side of the road here, edifices of nothing but scorching hot rock and prickly cactus.

As he slowed down his interest was sparked—there was an attractive young hippie girl outside trying to wave him down. For crying out loud, the van had California plates on it! She must either be lost or some nature worshipper out to hike in the Guadalupes and take in the back road sights as well. Oh well, too bad for her, he thought.

The intensity of the moment only grew as he passed slowly by, signaling to stop in front of her. Oh, my, she was a hotty—skin-tight, faded old bell bottom jeans, a halter top tied up that exposed her navel, and it was obvious she was bra-less. She wore a bright-colored headband, sunglasses, and a peace sign necklace. He would give her some peace alright. And this one was a blonde, he loved raping blondes—more of a novelty than the numerous Latino girls he had defiled and murdered. In his warped mind, he thought it were as though she was practically begging him to rape and abuse her. Perhaps he would make her beg him to abuse her—to spare her life. Not that he would, of course—but he would give her a shred of hope only to prolong her misery and lengthen his pleasure. Such thoughts were arousing him beyond control as his mind raced and he clutched his groin. He pulled over and turned off his engine. He could clearly see there was no one ahead of him for miles, and he had noted for some time that no one was behind him as well. Wow! California plates—no one would even miss this little piece of meat for who knows how long! How stupid this little hippie slut was to have traveled alone out here. At this point, Salvador was so aroused that even if she did have a male companion, he would simply kill him and dispose of them both later.

"What's the problem there, young lady?" he asked with impeccable English as he doffed his Stetson hat.

"My name is Sal Quionnes," he offered with his hands behind his back to falsely indicate that he was too unassuming of a gentleman to even offer to shake her hand. His face had a big, pleasant smile adorned with brilliant white teeth and a clean shave.

"Hi, Sal, my name is Cassie. My van just started sputtering and killed out," she explained, "I think I must've gotten some bad gas. Could you take a look at it?"

Cassie poised herself to sport her cleavage and protrude her buttocks just so to entice this rat. She felt as though she was convincingly naïve, although the palms of her hands were sweating and her heart was racing. She wasn't sure if maybe her voice had cracked a little, but then, it wouldn't be unusual to sound nervous around a perfect stranger out in the middle of nowhere.

With tremendous restraint, Salvador pretended not to notice this enticing beauty who was getting him terribly riled up in a sensual way. He refrained from staring or undressing her with his eyes—he was a master of deception with speech, voice tone, and body language.

"Good grief, little lady, you mean you're out here all alone?"

"Yes, I'm afraid I am. I'm going to some friends in Albuquerque but wanted to check out the Guadalupes on the way."

"I see, I see," he replied. "So where are you from in California?" he continued, savoring the moment and trying to bridle his sexual urges.

"Orange County—outskirts of LA."

"Los Angeles, really? I've been there lots of times. I have some cousins that live there. What a big place that is. Makes El Paso look small!" he smiled.

"When do you plan on getting to Albuquerque?" he queried, pretending to troubleshoot her engine as he peered all about under the hood.

"Oh, not for a couple of days," she invited, knowing he was seeking information to use to his advantage.

Salvador wiped his hands on his blue jeans then closed the hood with a bang. He glanced around at the road in both directions, pleased that no traffic could be seen.

"You're not going to Albuquerque or anywhere else, you slutty little bitch-whore!" he shouted as he slapped her face with a backhand knocking her into the side of the van. His hand had caught her on the ear and it was instantly ringing. Beneath her closed eyelids she actually saw multi-colored flashes of light as her head slammed hard into the side of the van. The bang on the metal was loud, and she imagined, of all things, that her head may have dented it in somewhat from the force. There was a distinct, painful, high-pitched ringing in her ear that wouldn't stop. She was instantly shocked by the extreme and excessive brute force and power he had mercilessly inflicted upon her. He grabbed her by the hair on the back of her head and snatched her to her feet.

"I'm going to teach you a little lesson about slutting around the country by yourself, you stupid little slut!" he shouted, his pulse racing and his eyes glazing.

"Put your hands behind your back! Hurry up before I beat the shit out of you, bitch!"

Horrified, Cassie complied, fearful that things were going too far, and that her rescuers might fail in their endeavor.

He roughhoused her to the back of the van and screamed at her to open the rear doors. This was not part of the plan. The plan by Knox had been for him to force her into his vehicle, not hers!

Knox was, in fact, hiding inside the van in a storage area underneath the built-in bed. His pulse quickened as he heard the struggle just inches away from him. Quionnes nearly ripped the blouse off Cassie and threw her into the back of the van on the bed, trapping Knox underneath. In an insane frenzy, Quionnes ripped at her jeans trying to pull them down. Knox pushed up on the access door, but the weight of the two was on top of him! He wanted to shout, but didn't know what would happen next! Joe Mack was just up the slope in the rocks, he would see what was going on, but he was some distance off; hopefully, he could get there before the damage was done. This animal had exploded with such unpredictable speed and ferocity!

CHAPTER 29

No Greater Love is This...

Percy Whitmore, Arlo McIntyre, and a couple of Rangers had been camped out far above the scene at some distance away, their vehicles stashed off the road in the backcountry and camouflaged. McIntyre, to Whitmore's chagrin, had been retained for his marksmanship skills. That sneaky private detective, Knox, had given Percy little warning about the plot and no means to shut it down. McIntyre had his scoped 30:06 Springfield honed in on the van, his face and forearms sweating, partly from the heat and partly from anticipation.

"For God sake, don't get over-zealous and shoot the young lady," Whitmore scolded.

"You want to take the shot?" McIntyre challenged, seething.

"Just keep a cool head and don't squeeze that trigger without communicating first with me. I'm the law here," Whitmore reminded him in no uncertain terms.

Charlie Knox instantly had visions of Cassie being raped before anyone could come to the rescue; he saw nothing else to do but start kicking up on the trap door of the bed and shouting.

Surprised and startled, Quionnes paused in his lustful passion. A trap! Damn it all, this was some sort of a trap! He got to his knees and pulled up his jeans, preparing for his escape as Knox moved the screaming and crying Cassie up and down on the trap door. She rolled to the side to provide for his exit as Quionnes zipped up his jeans. Once again, he jerked her by the hair and pulled her out of the van, cognizant that he might need a human shield to facilitate his escape.

Joe Mack had observed from upslope with his binoculars that something had gone south with Knox's plan. Damn! The monster had pulled his wife into the van, and he could quickly see that Knox would be pinned down beneath the trap door. They had planned on Quionnes taking Cassie to his vehicle and to nail him for assault with intent to do harm, kidnapping, and numerous other charges.

Joe Mack suddenly didn't care about logic, the plan, the backups who didn't even realize he was out here, or anything else. He loved that lady—she was his wife—and he would not allow her to be violated sexually by this savage predator. He scrambled down the slope as quickly as he could, dodging lechaguilla and agave plants lest they impale him right through his boots.

Upslope Whitmore heard the rock scrabble much to his surprise. He looked through his binoculars unable to believe his eyes! What the heck was Joe Mack doing out here on this operation? Why didn't Knox fill him in on this little detail? Damn it all, this had become complicated! His mind had not been in the best of form when he was contacted at the hospital late the night before about Knox's plan. He had barely had time to rendezvous and set up their lookout point up on the mountain. That it was a good plan to trap this vermin, he had no doubt, but he would have appreciated more time. He had figured Joe Mack was holed up in Carlsbad or someplace, not brought along for the ride out here. Trooper Jim Conklin was up the road a way in case the piece of rat filth escaped to the north, and the Hudspeth County sheriff's staff was over to the west a short distance, waiting in a hay shed monitoring their radio.

"Get ready to take the shot!" Whitmore shouted, no longer caring if he could be heard far down below or not.

McIntyre did not respond, but adjusted his body with his eye fixed on the scope and his finger touching the trigger of the rifle.

Quionnes had pulled a handgun from out of the back pocket of his jeans and held it to Cassie's head as he forced her along to his truck. Knox had exploded out of the back of the van, but Quionnes warned him to back off or he would kill Cassie. Quickly they scrambled toward the monster's truck, tears streaming down Cassie's cheeks and blood seeping from her swollen lower lip.

Quionnes paused when he heard Joe Mack scrambling down the slope and, in a flurry of desperation, fired off several rounds in his direction in the hope of shooting yet another surprise stranger. Joe

Mack ducked behind a rock, then lifted up his hat with a piece of ocatillo stalk. Several more shots rang out, one of them actually clipping the hat. Had his head been in it, that might have ended things in a tragic way.

Joe Mack was no novice to combat or lead projectiles coming his way. He noted that the monster was using a revolver, and by his count, he had expended six rounds. He had perhaps sixty to seventy yards of rough ground to cover before he reached the road, and Quionnes would have to reload.

Like a cornered lion up in a tree at the edge of a cliff, Quionnes loosed his grip on Cassie who slumped to the ground in shock. Quickly his fished a couple of cartridges out of his pocket to put in the cylinder. There was no time to fully reload, but he must stop his pursuers or kill the girl.

"Hold it—that's Joe Mack coming down the slope!" Whitmore ordered. For a reprehensible moment, an evil thought invaded his mind: What if Joe Mack accidentally got killed? Could he then be legitimately freed up to pursue his romantic notions with his widow? The better man within him prevailed and he yelled to McIntyre, "Stand down!"

"Stand down, nothing!" McIntyre barked as his finger started to squeeze on the trigger. Through his scope he could see the monster reloading his pistol and knew what the outcome would likely be.

"Damn it, man, you might hit the girl!" Whitmore shouted.

Arlo was frozen solid as his finger squeezed just tight enough on the trigger.

With a crack of thunder, the rifle exploded, even moving his massive shoulder a bit from the recoil.

With tears streaming down his face and a prayer on his lips, Charlie Knox ran to Cassie Mack's rescue "Lord, please don't let her die or suffer due to my error in judgment!" he pleaded aloud.

Knox had his revolver in his hand but didn't want to risk shooting Cassie, over whom Quionnes was now kneeling. Should Quionnes be killed, they may not have enough evidence to clear Joe Mack.

Almost in a blind panic, a badly out of shape Charlie Knox sprinted toward them. In his peripheral vision, he saw Joe Mack on the run and feared for his safety as well. Charlie rushed up to grab hold of the revolver Quionnes had just finished chambering more rounds into. Charlie felt the impact of something terribly powerful rip through his back and go clean through him before he heard the thunderous report of the rifle. The bullet kept going, leaving a much larger exit wound through his chest and tore into the right shoulder of Quionnes, causing him to drop the gun and recoil in anguish on the ground. A spray of blood had fairly well coated the faces and upper bodies of Quionnes and Cassie. For a moment, Charlie was not comprehending that the blood spatter everywhere was primarily from him. One lung was gone, and the gravity of the situation hit him at last.

"Cassie!" Charlie gasped. His voice was filled with so desperate a tone, such concern, such inquiry.

"Are you okay?" he asked as he slumped to the ground.

It was nearly impossible for Cassie to suppress her sobbing as Joe Mack pounced on Quionnes and started beating his face. The sick mad man laughed maniacally at him as though demon possessed.

Another shot rang out and dirt kicked up near the two men in struggle. Joe Mack immediately let Quionnes go and pulled Cassie to safety in the road ditch.

"You damned fool!" Whitmore shouted as he kicked the rifle from McIntyre's hands. What the hell are you doing?" Percy drew down on the tracker and ordered him to place his hands behind his back. What happened below would just have to play out for now. This whole operation was unraveling in directions it shouldn't have taken.

McIntyre belligerently refused and Whitmore shot a round so close to his head that fragments of rock cut Arlo's face. He quickly complied then, and Percy cuffed him and left him as he scrambled down the slope.

"Stand down, everyone—stand down!" Percy shouted as he scrambled down the

slope. From this distance, he wasn't sure what damage was done, but he was pretty sure

Knox wouldn't be going home alive.

Joe Mack came up cautiously with Cassie out of the road ditch and kicked Quionnes a couple of times hard in the ribs, then they went to Charlie Knox's side.

Blood was frothing from Charlie's mouth, and his eyes were welled up with tears. There was so much blood everywhere; his chest was covered with it. The rifle slug had hit him in the back and gone through one of his lungs. He wouldn't last long; that was for sure.

"Are you...two...kids...all right?" Charlie gasped.

Cassie couldn't speak, but nodded her head profusely in the affirmative, tears streaming down her face, clutching at her damaged, blood-spattered blouse to cover herself.

"Oh, Charlie!" Joe Mack exclaimed, tears running down his own cheeks. In short order he had come to love this man who had risked everything to bring about closure in this young couple's life.

"I'm...glad...you're all right," Charlie gasped, then continued, "It's okay, honey, it's okay. Charlie's going home... to be with... Jesus today! No...more worries...I love you kids!'

His eyes were looking distant; he tried to sit up a bit and pointed to something unseen on the other side of the road.

"No," Cassie pleaded, "Just rest, you're going to be all right, Charlie, you've got to be all right! I love you, Charlie!" she cried.

Somewhat incoherent, Charlie tried once again to point and whispered, "Let's cross over the river...and rest...'neath the shade tree..."

And with that, he lay back and his eyes closed as his last breath joined the hot West Texas wind for the final time.

Breathless, and feeling both ashamed and relieved, Percival Pinkerton Whitmore arrived on the scene. He could only nod his head initially in greeting to Joe Mack. He placed his hands on his thighs and inhaled slowly, trying to recuperate.

In the background, Quionnes continued to rant on and on about all the bitches he had raped and murdered, including that "stupid little Flores girl," and laugh like a maniac. Whitmore drew his pistol and aimed it at the madman at pointblank range, but he only laughed all the louder and begged him to pull the trigger. Percy wanted to waste the vermin right on the spot—without hesitation. His trigger finger strained; there seemed equal effort between trying to go ahead and squeeze off the shot and a presence of force to resist that very endeavor. Sweat was beaded heavily on his brow and his eyes were glazed with fury. With reluctance, Whitmore uncocked the hammer on his revolver, holstered his sidearm, and handcuffed the injured killer, wounded shoulder or not.

So much was thought, so much was apparent as the three looked down on Charlie Knox as he breathed his last. After a painful hesitation, Whitmore spoke.

"*Greater love hath no man than this, that a man lay down his life for his friends.*" That's a far better man lying there than me." And with an expression of guilt, shame and tears in his eyes, Percy Whitmore unpinned his badge and tossed it in the dirt beside Charlie Knox. He knelt down on the road and caressed his fallen comrade's brow.

"God forgive me for ever looking down upon the likes of you," Percy muttered.

Conklin and Slaughter arrived on the scene to haul off Quionnes. His time on this earth would be limited, but not before he repeatedly bragged and glorified himself for numerous despicable crimes. McIntyre and Joe Mack were arrested, although Joe Mack would soon be released on bond and his name cleared.

Overhead a group of turkey vultures floated high in the sky with the images of Guadalupe and El Capitan peaks in the background. There would be no meal here today, but death had occurred on a tragic scale.

Cassie thought for just a moment that she saw some other type of dark, winged creatures fluttering somewhat bat-like near Quionnes, but then they were gone. Probably the trauma she had endured playing tricks on her mind. The creatures appeared quite large, like winged men. Had she really seen them? Was she seeing something in the spirit? Perhaps not, but her flesh crawled anyway.

To the east, a mysterious figure was standing on the top of Shumard Peak on the western escarpment of the Guadalupes, looking toward the general direction where numerous gunshots could faintly be heard, though miles away. The sounds would have been inaudible to normal ears, but then he was no normal man. He wore a cloth head wrap, loin sash, and a carved wooden cross that hung by a leather lanyard around his neck. The barefooted throwback to the Apache took out his knife and slashed a cut across his chest, blood seeping down his trunk. He mimicked an anguished cry, although no sound emitted from his throat. He lifted his arms and looked up to the sky, apparently in some sort of prayer. He was seen by no one save God.

Cassie rode to El Paso with Joe Mack, who was not in handcuffs but under arrest just the same. Cassie rode up front with Ranger Whitmore, who tended to stare straight ahead up the highway. Once or twice their eyes met with a certain uneasiness, but it was difficult to exchange any words. Halfway there, she reached out her hand toward his and placed his Ranger badge back into Percy's hand. She smiled a knowing smile, and let him know through silence and facial expression that he was forgiven, and that she was grateful for his service.

"I'll use every bit of influence I have to clear this mess up for you, Joe," Whitmore offered, relieved at the righteousness of the outcome—at least for their sakes, though not for Charlie Knox...

CHAPTER 30

Will The Circle Be Unbroken?

The funeral was sparsely attended at Pastor Jack Shafer's church. The ride to the tiny ranch of Joe and Cassie Mack would take longer than the service did. There were few there to hear the profound service that Pastor Jack fervently shared that day. There were a couple of local police officers and their wives, Charlie's landlady, a couple of waitresses from his favorite café, and Percy and Helen Whitmore.

Pastor Jack shared from his King James Bible in John 14, verses 1 through 6:

"*Let not your heart be troubled: ye believe in God, believe also in me. In my father's house are many mansions: if it were not so I would have told you. I go to prepare a place for you. And if I go and prepare a place for you, I will come again and receive you unto myself; that where I am there ye may be also. And whither I go ye know, and the way ye know. Thomas said unto him, Lord we know not whither thou goest; and how can we know the way? Jesus saith unto him, I am the way, the truth and the life: no man cometh to the Father but by me.*"

"You know, friends and loved ones," Pastor Jack continued, "Cassie and Joe asked me about something Charlie said when he died. When they shared it, I thought it familiar, so I did a little research at the local library. Either Charlie was better read than we assumed, or else he otherwise uttered something which parallels another famous figure in the history of our great nation. Charlie's last words in effect were: *"Let us cross over the river and rest in the shade of the trees."* This is almost verbatim from Stonewall Jackson as he lay dying after a mortal wound during the Civil War. Historians may dispute his character, but no military man will dispute his genius, and no Christian would ever dispute the purity of his faith..."

Percy Whitmore held Helen's hand during the service as tears cleansed his eyes and his spirit. Something was igniting in his soul with his wife, and the feeling was mutual. They would have much to talk about on the drive to the ranch near where the shoot-out at Salt Flat occurred.

It had rained hard up in the Guadalupes just before the entourage arrived at Mack's ranch. It presented one of those rare times when there was actually a shallow stand of water in the salt lakes on the west side of the escarpment. The mountains were reflected in placid lake like a mirror. The sun would be setting in another hour or so. The solemn procession noted the rain-washed environment, how clean everything was for a while, sort of fresh and new. It was the golden time of the day.

Suddenly, Joe Mack spotted a four o'clock bush alongside the road and pulled over, disrupting the procession. Normally he saw them higher up in the mountains; they were by far his and Cassie's favorite flower. They had dark green, almost waxen-looking leaves and numerous fuchsia-colored flowers. They were incomprehensibly beautiful. Perhaps they were a sign from God that He had received Charlie's spirit. He admired the beauty of the flowers and, ironically, somehow the beauty of the moment.

Charlie would be buried on Cassie and Joe Mack's tiny ranch, and his marker would be a reminder of the noblest of deeds that anyone had ever done for them. Helen and Percy would have a lengthy and profound—even healing—conversation with the vibrant pastor after a wonderful home-cooked meal at the Macks. Jim Conklin would stop by for the graveside service in his uniform, for he was on duty.

Shockingly, the young priest—ex-priest now—Mike Arias was present as well. He had been following the case on television and in the newspapers and made many petitions in prayer on their regard. Although he wrestled with the status of his religion, he did not doubt the power of the one true God.

The Flores couple was there, having found some sense of closure now that the monster who had raped and murdered their daughter had been apprehended. Their healing would be difficult and, in fact, they would never totally get over the loss of their only child. In a different way, they had something tragic in common with Percy and Helen Whitmore.

In some sort of symbolic gesture, there were three riders with tall black cowboy hats and matching duster jackets that went nearly to their boots mounted on horseback; they were further back from the rest of the party and were framed with the prominent backdrop of that Permian fault line feature, the Guadalupe Mountains with the prominent peaks of El Capitan, Guadalupe Peak, Shumard, and Bush Mountain easily recognizable in the late afternoon skyline. At this time of the day, the sunlight would reflect in shades of crimson, purple, or golden on the stark limestone cliffs. It was the golden time of the day. Although not necessary, their horses were equipped in addition to the necessary tack gear with lassos and bedrolls. Beside the trio of somewhat mysterious riders was one riderless mount, Blackjack, equipped with saddle, bridle, even a bedroll and lasso on the saddle horn, and a black duster coat draped over the saddle. Perhaps it was an indicator that Charlie was being posthumously accepted through his association with Joe and Cassie Mack into the local family of cowboys, who, if they could, would escort him into eternity on that big cattle drive up in the sky.

Three of Joe Mack's friends were beside the grave with their guitars and Sunday best; they sang a few songs Charlie would have approved of. Among them were *Blue Eyes Crying in the Rain* and *Will The Circle Be Unbroken?*

There are loved ones in the glory,
whose dear forms you often miss;
when you close your earthly story,
will you join them in their bliss?
Will the circle be unbroken,
By and by, by and by,

In a better home awaiting,
In the sky, Lord, in the sky...
In the joyous days of childhood,
Oft they told of wondrous love,
Pointed to the dying Savior,
Now they dwell with him above...

Cassie and Joe Mack had provided the burial plot, Pastor Jack had provided the service, and Percy and Helen Whitmore had insisted on providing the marble marker. Underneath Charlie's name was the scripture, "*Greater love hath no man than this, that a man lay down his life for his friends.*"

Just after the gentlemen from the funeral home had lowered Charlie's casket into the ground and started to bury it, Helen Whitmore pulled a pint bottle of whiskey from her purse. It had been partially consumed. She started to unscrew the cap, and Pastor Jack looked at her incredulously.

"For crying out loud, is she going to propose a toast and take a pull of that vile stuff right here at poor Charlie's graveside?" he wondered.

Pastor Jack restrained himself and said nothing for the moment. Helen Whitmore dumped the whiskey out into the ground and tossed the empty bottle into his partially filled grave, "Thank you, Charlie, thank you for initiating a turning point in many of our miserable lives. I wish I had known you, I wish..." she trailed off as tears streamed down her cheeks.

A dust devil kicked up some of the powdery dry West Texas soil and swirled it skyward perhaps a couple of hundred feet. A red-tailed hawk perched on a nearby fencepost overlooking the domain surrounded by barbed wire, looking for something to prey upon, something to eat. The hawk cocked its head curiously as it looked toward the trailer house and corrals and barn, and the people engaged in some sort of activity outside. The raptor cast but a fleeting, curious glance at the peculiar dung beetle rolling a ball of cow manure larger than itself on the ground below. The bizarre custodian of the insect world was rolling the fecal sphere to a location to be later used for food. It was oblivious to everything around it, seemingly clumsy in its task as it both rolled and was at times rolled with the dung and dust.

As he clutched his wife's hand in his, Joe Mack looked in the direction of the hawk, which seemed to pick up on being observed, then reluctantly and somewhat nonchalantly took to the air and flew away. Joe Mack mused how like the spirit of Charlie Knox this hawk must be, drifting carefree on the currents of the West Texas winds with the majestic Guadalupe Mountains as a backdrop; he wondered if Charlie had been lifted skyward from Crow Flats up toward the heavens, going over the top of El Capitan and the Guadalupe peaks where Charlie had likely never been—just to give him a bird's eye view of some of the wonders God had created...

Ten months later, Joseph Charles Mack was born.

Art by Mike Capron

SHOOT-OUT AT SALT FLAT

Afterword

In the fall of 1986, my wife, Belinda, and I moved from the Quinault rain forest of Olympic National Park in Washington state, where we averaged 150 inches of annual rainfall to the Guadalupe Mountains of West Texas, where we might get about 18 inches in the high country and only 10 inches in nearby El Paso. It was Texas's Sesquicentennial year—150 years in existence! We had been married just four years, and yet, all of a sudden, a love affair began for me. That love affair was with the Guadalupes—a mountain range arguably less spectacular than many others, and yet there was something irresistible, inviting, about it. Most people either hate that part of the country or fall in love with it; obviously, I was the latter. My predecessor at Guadalupe Mountains National Park and his wife, I am told, lasted only about a month or two before leaving the lonely, isolated area of West Texas. A similar, more radical story, was of the bride at the Williams Ranch on the west side leaving after only a night!

We eventually purchased 50 acres of what could fairly be described as rocky, brushy, cactus-strewn wasteland which is barely inhabitable to desert hares and lizards. It's perhaps worthless other than being in close proximity of the national park in the Patterson Hills with a spectacular view of the west side of the escarpment. We eventually sold a 20-acre parcel and still have an L-shaped 30-acre parcel that we rarely even visit. Many people have stated that they somehow feel different in that backcountry, like there is something almost spiritual there. Perhaps there is; after all, ancient civilizations believed they could get closer to God by going up on a high mountain.

Shootout at Salt Flat had to happen. It had to happen because this significant part of West Texas had, at best, brief references in so many full-length or dime-store novels. Just think—the Butterfield Stage ran through there, the Buffalo Soldiers and the Mescalero Apache did battle there, treasure seekers explored there, and years later, bandits took refuge there. To me, there needed to be some sort of a Western that depicted those prominent peaks—El Capitan and Guadalupe—on the book cover. These peaks are geological features as recognizable in West Texas as Chimney Rock is in Western Nebraska. Both peaks, although primarily Guadalupe, have locally been described as Signal Peak over the years by locals in reference to the Mescalero Apache sending up smoke signals to warn of approaching US Cavalry or other possible adversaries back in the days of Western settlement. Both were easily recognizable landmarks to Westward travelers and continue to inspire reflection to this very day. Although this story is a contemporary Western, the mission is now accomplished, at least to my frame of mind.

Once I had this manuscript finished and the artwork and foreword in progress, I came across some old correspondence with a great Western writer whom I knew and admired: the late Elmer Kelton. I have a copy of a letter I wrote to him, and his response to me—about basing a Western novel in the Guadalupes. I lobbied and begged him to write one, as I knew of no one more articulate, respected, and qualified for such a piece. In paraphrase, Elmer wrote back that perhaps someone would write such a novel, just not him. He was getting too old, travel had become a struggle, and his writing career had entered its twilight era.

I had first met Elmer in San Angelo, Texas, on April 23, 1994, while attending the Buffalo Soldier stamp dedication at Fort Concho. Although Elmer was not at Fort Concho, I had found him listed in the phone book and called him to see if he would autograph a copy of *The Wolf and the Buffalo*, which he had written. He graciously agreed and came to the motel where I and my young son, Cody, were staying. I couldn't even buy the man a cup of coffee! He told us he had already had breakfast. He graciously signed my book and allowed the waitress to take a photograph of us together. It was pretty early, and Cody looked half asleep in the picture. Four years later, Elmer came to a symposium I arranged called the African American Military Experience Symposium (AAMES) in Carlsbad, New Mexico, and participated in the book-signing portion of the event, which was hosted by the Eddy County Detachment of the Marine Corps League.

I had wished to have Elmer review this manuscript, but that was not to happen. No doubt, he would have, he was that unimposing, that gracious, that giving and humble. I can by no means compare the content of this story to the mastery that Elmer possessed, but I mention him because he has been an inspiration to me for many years and I have learned much by reading his books and listening to some of his writing seminars on audio cassette.

In my fantasies, I wish I had completed the manuscript sooner and convinced him to write the foreword. Instead, I take solace in the fact that I may likely have the last autograph he did from his hospital bed on the December/January edition of *American Cowboy Magazine,* which featured an article on Elmer when he had been voted "All Time Best Western Author" by the Western Writers of America. John Wayne was on the front cover, and Elmer signed the cover, as well as inside. At the time, I didn't know his health had declined or that he was hospitalized. I had mailed the magazine off a long time prior, and it had remained on his desk at home. Only when I wrote a follow-up inquiry had Elmer's daughter searched his desk at home and taken it to him at the hospital. I'd had no idea he was having severe health problems or had been hospitalized. Rest assured, I treasure that magazine. Later, I took one of Elmer's paperback books, *The Eye of the Hawk*, with me on an arduous trek up El Capitan with my son Cody in the southern edge of the Guadalupes in Elmer's honor. I inscribed something to that effect inside the cover on El Capitan and smeared a little dust from the peak on it for good measure. It just seemed like a cowboy thing to do.

Larry Henderson, retired, former superintendent of Guadalupe Mountains National Park, was the next best logical pick to write the foreword. Larry personally knows another writer, Nevada Barr, who wrote a murder mystery novel based in the Guadalupes called *Track of the Cat*, which was published in 1993. Ms. Barr had spent some time in the Guadalupes when Larry was superintendent. In fact, Larry and his wife, Signe, recently had dinner with Nevada Barr and her husband in Tucson, Arizona. Ms. Barr was the recipient of the first Stewart Udall Award by the Western National Parks Association at their 75th anniversary celebration in Tucson in 2013.

Larry was career Park Service and particularly loved the Guadalupes and the nearby town of Carlsbad, New Mexico. What's more, he knows me, as we worked together for a number of years at Guadalupe, where I was the Buildings and Utilities supervisor. Larry's love of history and the great outdoors is without question. He is in many ways an expert by exposure, research, and interest in history and science as it pertains to this region of the country. He appreciates people of character and has a great passion for the written word.

It's funny how our lives are threaded together. At the symposium Elmer attended, I also met Bonnie Curnock, who did the artwork for our brochures for the AAME Symposium. Bonnie over the years has worked in many national parks as a cave-preservation specialist and has done professional artwork in many venues, including being the lead painter in a Billy Bob Thornton movie, *Crystal.* I had lost contact with her for 12 years or better, but I believe it was a God thing that my wife Belinda tracked her down through the Internet, even though I had previously tried. Bonnie is an attention-to-details kind of artist and has been in the Guadalupes and Carlsbad Caverns. Thanks to her, one of the minor characters in the book had a name change. Also thanks to her, I described the Soaptree Yucca in the shootout scene which I had envisioned in my mind but failed to impart it to the reader! I had originally dubbed the '52 Chevy pickup truck Old Blue, in keeping with the name I'd had for my old 1968 Plymouth Belvedere years ago. (As I recall, I cried when I finally sold that old car.) For the sake of aesthetics, and contrast, the truck needed to be red to "pop" on the jacket art, so I changed the name of him to Old Red. One may not judge a book by the cover, but to me and many like me, the cover art plays an important role. After all, I had on occasion in my youth purchased some Edgar Rice Burroughs novels, attracted first by the fantastic art of Frank Frazetta. Bonnie was familiar with that artist as well, and I could tell some funny stories about the evolution of the art piece on this book.

As somewhat of an afterthought, I contacted Mike Capron from Texas, a longtime cowboy, ranch manager, and professional artist, to do an interior sketch, just because he is such a neat person and I wanted to include someone of his caliber in this piece. He is an expert on the location that I am writing about and has been a great motivational person in this endeavor. Mike has done book illustrations professionally a number of times during his career, in addition to creating stand-alone western art that is spectacular and well-known throughout the region. I thought it would be an honor to include him in at least some small way.

In summation to the story, it is a composite of characters and instances that I have gathered in the highways and bi-ways of my memory and molded into something of a contemporary Western soap opera, a manhunt kind of tale. Although the characters are all fictional, I have been inspired by many characters in my lifetime. As I often say, "Some people are just people, and then there are *characters!*" The characters with all with their flaws and weaknesses, even the unlikely heroes such as Charlie Knox. This is definitely a lesson I learned from Elmer Kelton, who also once said, "Western writers are liars and thieves!" Guilty as charged! The character name Charlie Knox, I once read in,of all things, a science fiction story by Harlan Ellison. The characters are in no way alike, but the name stuck in my mind, and I couldn't help using it.

Only my wife, Belinda, of more than 30 years, and perhaps a very few people who know me well could pick out some parallels to my own life, or the lives of others I have known, yet to some extent, as the story progressed—now don't think me superstitious—the characters seemed to run away with the plot and evolve as they damn well pleased. Elmer Kelton wrote about this phenomenon, and I must concur, it is true.

What are true, for the most part, are historical references and the descriptions and nomenclature of the flora and fauna, geology and history. I have hiked and traveled that West Texas and Southeast New Mexico country extensively, and a portion of my heart is forever branded with poignant memories and a burning love for that section of this great United States of America and the characters who have inhabited it. Until my dying day, it will be the home of my dreams, whether or not I ever return to it. That region will be emblazoned on my heart as long as there is a dominant and incessant West Texas wind. I hope this book will be held special and dear to anyone who has ever experienced the Guadalupes, West Texas, or Southeast New Mexico.

If I mention a song or a product in the book, it is indeed from that era. When I researched songs for authenticity, I came to realize how much more profound, intelligent, patriotic, and inspirational the songs from that era were than they are now. Many cried out from tortured hearts about things they had a great deal of passion for. Besides, if this book were ever to be made into a movie, what a great soundtrack it could have, appreciated especially by baby boomers like myself!

I certainly want to thank my wife, Belinda, for being an encouragement to me in this lifetime dream; Larry Henderson, Bonnie Curnock, and Mike Capron for their contributions; T. K. Kajiki at the Carlsbad Caverns & Guadalupe Mountains Association for giving me a chance for a market on this endeavor; and Miles Nelson at Dog Ear Publishing for all his gracious encouragement and direction.

It is my fervent hope and prayer that the obstacles the characters overcome in this story somehow inspire each of you who have struggles and challenges of your own. It is enough to spin a yarn but is far more desirable to be able to inspire and give hope and passion in the content. After all, as the Bible says, "there is no greater love than a man would lay down his life for a friend." Forgiveness is one of the most challenging and life-changing choices we can make, and some of the most simple pleasures in this world don't cost a dime, only our momentary pause and appreciation.

Lynn Chelewski
April 22, 2013

Somewhere in Nebraska

CPSIA information can be obtained at www.ICGtesting.com
Printed in the USA
LVOW08s0800230814

400577LV00002B/4/P